Annette Langer's trials and tribulations will bring a tear to your eye as her ever-present positive outlook will bring a smile to your face. Langer is a master at finding a mountain of mirthful moments in her major and minor mishaps. Read this book, learn from her, and you, too, will be healed through humor!

Allen Klein
Author and President of the Association for Applied and Therapeutic Humor

Annette Langer's joy, grace and zest for living despite her own challenges shine through on every page. "Healing Through Humor" is a treasure of personal stories that demonstrates how to face life's adversities with spunk and wit.

Kathy Cordova
Author and Producer/Co-Host of Cable TV's "In a Word"

Annette Langer takes the reader along on her journey through her many illnesses, accidents and injuries, and there *are* some funny twists and turns on the way! A firm believer in the role humor plays in the healing process, she demonstrates through her personal trials how to accept some measure of responsibility in one's own recovery from disease or disability. Langer's words are an art form used to paint her stories, drawing readers into a vivid world of warmth, humor and healing. This is a "must read" for patient and caregiver alike!

Pat Goard
RN Practitioner

No one likes being ill or injured, and not everyone possesses the ability to "spit in the eye" of adversity. But, this book will point you in the right direction and give you the tools. Annette Langer's stories never fail to give one a glimpse of climbing to the other side of hard times and holding onto the gift of laughter while making that journey. Having cared for seriously ill patients in hospitals and in private settings, I've seen first hand how humor eases the way and facilitates more rapid healing. Langer is a survivor and will help you to be one, too, providing a good laugh in the process.

Judy Hanneman
Registered Nurse

Whether you're trying to comfort or guide someone through sickness, health or *any* tough time, this book has an answer. I can take some of Langer's stories and apply them to the rough spots in my own life, healthy or not. No matter what the situation, Langer's funny and comforting manner can be addressed to any problem. It's a wonderful book, a book for a friend in need—a friend in *any* need.

Mona Dawson
Travel Consultant

I thought about reading a couple chapters of the book for starters, but I just couldn't put it down! It's such great reading—funny in all the right places, but also inspiring. I'm able to apply some of Langer's words of wisdom to "stuff" happening in my own life. I can't wait to stock up on her book for my friends!

Sheila Heinrich
Account Supervisor

Healing Through Humor

Change Your Focus, Change Your Life!

Annette Langer

WingSpan Press

Cover Design: Robert Owen with permission
Interior Illustrations: Microsoft Office Online Media Elements©
Copyright 2005 Microsoft Corp.

Printed in the United States of America.

Published by
WingSpan Press
Livermore, CA
www.WingSpanpress.com

The WingSpan® name, logo and colophon are the trademarks
of WingSpan Publishing.

EAN 978-1-59594-025-4

ISBN 1-59594-025-1

First Edition 2005

Library of Congress Control Number: 2005934259

To everyone who is not yet healed—
May you find hope and
peaceful days ahead through humor.

ACKNOWLEDGEMENTS

This book is dedicated to everyone who ever made me laugh during my life (or kept me in "stitches" along the way).

I am grateful for the comments and suggestions of those who read early drafts of this book, ever encouraging me to put more of "myself" into the pages. Dear to me is Joanne Giampa who urged me to put my thoughts down on paper in the first place. She sent me over five hundred e-mails (from her "Annette" file that I had written to her over the years) to help jog my flagging memory and organize my thoughts in order to put them down on paper. Her insights, and the editorial comments of Pat Goard, Judy Hanneman, Donna Surace and Linnea Westlake, were invaluable to its successful completion.

Thanks also to the BMW's (whose name is fully explained in Chapter 15) for standing by me, comforting me throughout my challenges and showing me how to smile through song.

My love and thanks go to all my friends and family not named here, but especially to my sister, Dolores Jordan, who keeps me grounded and teaches me how to achieve that delicate balance between playfulness and somber reality.

I am especially grateful to David Collins, my editor, and his staff at WingSpan Press. His patience and talent breathed life into these pages, finally taming the beast of a manuscript into an organized, readable book.

Finally, my heartfelt gratitude goes to all the many doctors, physical therapists and other health care workers whose talents and skills have brought me to where I am today—still upright and taking nourishment. (I've disguised their identities in the book out of respect for their privacy. Who knows? I may decide to write a sequel someday and may need to use them again. Never burn your bridges!)

CONTENTS

PROLOGUE

Dear reader, take note from the outset. This is *not* going to be your typical "How to" health book. That sort of self-help book and the role it plays within the realm of health care and healing most often is based on observations of other people and their behaviors. Through case study, clinical trials, etc., etc., blah, blah, blah, that type of writing actually tells someone else's story. This book tells *my* story. What will unfold in the pages that follow are illustrations of how I discovered ways to cope with my own encounters with health issues, how I learned to minimize suffering and how I hope to share the "secrets" with you to apply them to challenges in your own life.

This book isn't intended to poke mean-spirited fun at the medical community (although I *have* taken some good-natured jabs here and there). I didn't write it to trivialize, for the sake of comedy, the very real problems that accompany many medical difficulties. And I haven't encumbered it with long quotations by scholarly types or perspectives of stodgy, health care pundits. (If it would bore me to write it, I'm sure it would bore you to read it, healthy or not.) For the sake of balance, though, I have sprinkled in here and there a few, brief observations of some very insightful "experts in living" in order to emphasize a particular point.

Over time, I've come to recognize that the key to "challenging the challenge" lies in a gift that each and every one of us has received in life (hopefully, more often than not), but whose value we probably take for granted most of the time. That gift is simply—everyday humor. Humor is one of the most commanding tools we have in our possession, both for its own enjoyment and sharing it with others, as well. Like a row of dominoes, it spills over and affects in some way whomever it touches.

Our perceptions of something and how we choose to react to it are many times all we really have control over in a seemingly hopeless situation. Everything we do or experience is part of a process through which we define ourselves and our circumstances. How we interpret our situations and how we react to them can make a profound impact on our assessment of the "big picture". If you have any doubt at all in the power of perceptions, here's an extreme example to demonstrate the point.

It's a tale about two young women who went to the local zoo one afternoon. A large sign posted outside the gorilla cage cautioned patrons to stay at a safe distance for their own protection. Ignoring the warning, the women stepped a little too close to the cage in order to get a better look. The gorilla, seizing the opportunity, suddenly reached out and grabbed one of them, dragging her through the bars. She was rescued by the zoo attendants but not before the gorilla "had his way with her"—right there on the floor of the cage.

The next day the other young woman went to visit her in the hospital. When she entered the room, she gazed at her friend lying there in the hospital bed. She just stared vacantly out the window, looking morose and forlorn.

"Oh, my dear," her friend sobbed. "Did he hurt you badly?"

"Did he *hurt* me?" the young woman lamented. "He doesn't write. He doesn't call. Of *course*, he hurt me!"

Silly? Sure. But it illustrates the point that a person's focus or narrow view of an event can have an overwhelming effect on one's entire evaluation of a situation. In a broader sense, if you define a circumstance as hopeless, you can make it so, just through your inability or unwillingness to see other aspects of the situation.

☞☜✦☞☜✦☜

My own story began back in 1962 as a teenager, the first time that I can remember staying overnight in a hospital. Yes, I really am that old. (Actually, I stopped celebrating birthdays the year my age exceeded my bra size, and that was a *very* long time ago.) But, that's a whole other story. The point here is that the most valuable lesson I've learned in my lifetime is that discovering the humor in a situation can probably help you through most anything, including coping with major illness or injury.

You might say that I learned to become part of my own healing through refocusing my outlook. That, in turn, affected my perceptions and appraisal of the circumstance. In essence, I've "softened the edges" of my sometimes battle with health issues, and humor has helped me to heal.

Much of the humor that I have found (or that has found me) as I journeyed along my path to healing is chronicled here in these chapters. It's the common thread that binds all of them together. I hope that in reading this book, you'll be entertained (which, in itself, can help distract you temporarily from your struggles) and that you may even discover a parallel to past events from your own life.

If you think that none of what follows could possibly apply to you or your current situation, begin by asking yourself: What's the best thing that's happened to me during the worst thing that's happened to me? What did I learn? What did I gain? Perhaps it was a small, isolated incident from your past, one that you barely gave any notice at the time, but one that turned out to be a powerful catalyst, a turning point. If you believe (at first) that nothing good has taken place, be patient. Sometimes it may not be immediately perceptible, or you may not have opened yourself up yet to seeing it.

It's all about patience and balance, tempering the bad aspects of any challenge by discovering the good, and exercising the control you may not even realize you possess. Allen Klein, noted author and President of the Association for Applied and Therapeutic Humor, cautions that all of your problems will *not* vanish if you laugh. But "...when you learn to spot some humor in your difficulties, you gain a new perspective that will help you deal with them".

If you choose to allow humor to help you heal from a serious physical illness or injury, keep in mind that I'm not suggesting in any way that it substitute conventional medical care.   But, when you let humor in *alongside* traditional forms of treatment, it can become a very powerful factor in the healing process.

CB&CRÐ&Ð

These are the "secret ingredients" that I hope you will use as your springboard to help you lighten the load and get through this and all the struggles of your life. Finding humor "rest stops" along the way is one of the simple pleasures that life offers us to provide that needed breather when you're overwhelmed with "negatives". It is the cumulative effect of those breathers that will give you the inner strength to help you face your adversity.

You may not be well enough yet to absorb more than a bit at a time as you're reading this. I purposely designed the chapters to be short, taking your stamina and attention span into consideration as I wrote them. Take a little of this and a little of that, and then think about it. See how it may apply to your own life, to your own personal trials. By the time you reach the end of this book, I hope you'll have recognized some of the balancing "positives" in your life. I hope your awareness will be heightened sufficiently in order to help you answer the "what's good about it?" question, as well as fashion a plan to help you move forward.

It is my wish that something you discover in these pages will lessen your burden for a time, help you shift your focus to the positive elements that accompany any struggle and teach you how to use this most compelling gift in your own life to help you heal. These are *my* funny stories. Take the time as you read them to remember your own. Everyone has them.

Please join me now for an hour, a week, a year, a lifetime.

Annette Langer

– ONE –

The Time I *Should* Have Died—But Didn't

Never lie to your parents. It always comes back to bite you in the butt, especially the big ones (lies, not butts). The short version of my biggest lie is that many years ago, I led my parents to believe I was going on a vacation to Wisconsin with a girlfriend. In truth, I was driving alone from my home in Chicago to a Marine Corps base in North Carolina to visit a boyfriend stationed there (whom they didn't like, of course). If I had known I'd end up in a head-on automobile collision on my way back home, almost losing my life, I'd never have made the trip, of course—teenage love be damned! But you don't expect this sort of ending to a love story (ha!), especially at age eighteen when you think you're invincible and know it all.

This took place in the days before safety laws requiring seat belts. Had I been wearing one at the time, you wouldn't even be reading this now, at least not written by me. My lightweight car ricocheted off the other car on impact, jumped the guardrail and slid down a snow-slicked, forty-foot embankment. It came to rest at the bottom on the railroad tracks, but not before the gas tank ruptured. (This almost reads like an action movie script, doesn't it?) I broke the front bench seat and flew like a human rocket into the back seat, smashing the right rear door open with my head. The engine ended up in the front seat where I would have been, had I been seat-belted.

I lay near death several yards away from where I had been launched, and my brand-new car was totaled—just a couple weeks after I had made the last payment on it. (Punishment for lying.) I suffered a *subdural hematoma* in the crash (a four-inch blood clot on the brain), severe whiplash, several lacerations and a fractured collarbone, not even discovered until years later on x-ray.

The small, North Carolina hospital in the town nearest to where the accident happened wasn't equipped to treat a severe head injury. So, I was transferred by *funeral hearse* (their version of an ambulance) to a larger hospital in the state of Virginia better equipped to treat me. Imagine my parents' confusion after being telephoned by someone with a heavy Southern accent from the Virginia hospital to let them know I had been in an auto accident in North Carolina (no, *not* Wisconsin), that I would require immediate, emergency brain surgery, and if I didn't have it, I could go blind or even die.

They were urged to make their flight arrangements but not buy the tickets yet. At that point, the neurosurgeon didn't know if he could even save me. If he couldn't, then my body would be "shipped" home, they were told.

Several hours passed, and in the middle of the night, the neurosurgeon called back and advised my folks to get there quickly because he didn't know how long he could keep me alive. I was even given the Last Rites, which is what the Catholic Church called it back then. Normally, if you got the Last Rites, you were pretty much a goner. Today, it's called the Sacrament of Healing or Anointing of the Sick so the new lingo doesn't freak people out so much. It can be given to anyone who is seriously ill but not necessarily in *imminent* danger of death. It's an anointing of the body with holy oils, accompanied by prayers said by a priest for the person's salvation and forgiveness of sins. (So much for the catechism lesson. Now, back to the story.)

Early the next morning, my folks took their *three* connecting flights from Chicago to reach Roanoke, Virginia. (What a time to introduce them to air travel!) They arrived late in the afternoon, went directly to the hospital Information Desk and introduced themselves.

The young girl behind the desk said in her sweetest Southern drawl, "Oh, *you're* the parents of the deceased."

My parents said, *"What?!!!"*

Then the girl covered and said, "Oh, I'm sorry. I meant the patient in a *coma*." (Wonder how long she worked *there* after making slips like that.)

My mother and dad found their way to my room but froze in their tracks a few yards from the door. It was closed and a small sign was posted on it. They were certain it meant that I had died after all and that my body was being "prepared". As they ventured closer, however, they were able to read the sign. It just cautioned that oxygen was being administered inside and requested anyone wishing to enter to knock first.

They didn't even recognize me after they did enter the room. An older woman was asleep in one bed while a young, dark-skinned girl lay motionless in an oxygen tent in another. My head was cocooned in a turban-like bandage from the surgery, and my face and body had turned black from bruising.

Over the days that passed, long, rigid splints had to be strapped to my arms to restrain them. That prevented me from bending my arms and pulling out the I.V.'s (which, apparently, I kept trying to do). Even while unconscious, I'm told I clawed at and then hit one nurse on the head with my splinted arm as she attended to me, almost knocking her out. (Oops! Sorry about that.)

I remained in a coma for ten days, and when I finally regained consciousness, I would discover that my fingernails had been clipped short, I was completely bald (my head having been shaved for the brain surgery), I had double vision, partial paralysis on one side of my body, no memory at all of having the accident, *and* no car. Later in my stay, I was shown photos taken by the insurance company representative of the crumpled mass that once was my precious, first car. (Tires looked okay.)

ৰ্জ কৃ ৫৪৪৪ কৃ৪৪

Roanoke Memorial Hospital was where I met Peggy whose mother, also a long-term patient, shared the hospital room with me. An extra cot had been set up for Peggy in our room because their home was too far away for her to make a regular commute to visit. My parents stayed at a tourist home in town, a private residence of a woman who rented out rooms to people going back and forth to the hospital.

Each day they'd take the local bus to the hospital, driven by the same bus driver who'd routinely ask, "How's your little girl doin' today?"

After I emerged from the coma and returned to "the land of the living", Peggy and I got to know each other and gradually formed a friendship, getting both of us through our respective crises. (We exchange Christmas cards to this day.) She would help feed me while her own mother slept, giving my mom a break. My dad had gone back to work in Chicago by that time, and my mother stayed on with me until I was released to go home finally, weeks later.

Peggy and I would talk for hours—about boys, our lives back home, the latest fashions, everything teenage girls talk about. She taught me Southern songs like the one by Guy Marks that went: *"Oh, your red scarf matches your eyes. You closed your cover before striking. Father had the shipfitter bluuuues. Loving you has made me bananas."* (It's better in person.) When she fed me, she said it was like "peeling grapes for Emperor Nero". The nickname, "Nero", stuck with me for years.

After Peggy's mother was discharged, I met other hospital patients who were close to my age. To pass the long days, we devised games to keep ourselves amused—like wheelchair races. I wasn't strong enough yet to participate in these contests, but I did accept the role as Official Starter, shouting "Go!" from my hospital bed as the boys careened down the hall to the "finish line" at the elevators. Our games were discouraged by the nursing staff, of course, and were finally put to a halt after "the incident".

On that fine, but fateful day, the sun was shining, the birds were singing in the trees outside, and the Nurse Capping Ceremony had just concluded. Happy nurses, family and friends poured out of the auditorium into the hallway just as two expert wheelchair racers rounded the corner. No one was seriously injured, but that put an end our "chariot" racing, once and for all.

I was working for the Social Security Administration at the time, and my office manager in Chicago had telephoned the manager of the Social Security office there in Roanoke. He asked if someone could come to visit me in the hospital to cheer me up since I was so far from home. A couple of people did visit, announcing from the doorway that they were from Social Security. My head was still in a fog from the surgery, subsequent coma and drugs, and it was hard to think straight. In my confusion, I was convinced that I really had died and that they were there to pay the Social Security death benefit!

The first time I tried to walk on my own power was a major event. It seemed as though the entire hospital staff had assembled for it and tried to crowd into the doorway of my room to watch. My handsome attending physician held out his arms to me and urged me forward. It would have made the perfect cover for a trashy romance novel (he was *hot!*) had it not been for the stupid hospital gown that kept trying to open while I shuffled a few steps toward him, wavered and then fell forward unexpectedly into his outstretched arms. Everyone applauded my small progress, he gave me a warm, encouraging hug, and I was ushered back to my bed. Baby steps.

While in the hospital all those weeks relearning how to walk, feed myself and regain my strength, I received over three hundred greeting cards in the mail. Many were from relatives, friends and co-workers, but a good number of them were from people from work whom I didn't even know. My office manager had sent out a memo to each department (that's a piece of paper we used in the caveman days before e-mail) notifying them of my accident and encouraging the employees to send get-well cards to brighten my days.

I celebrated my nineteenth birthday in the hospital, as well, and that generated even more good wishes. After sending all those greeting cards up to my room, the hospital mailroom supervisor paid me a visit, wanting to know who the "celebrity" was. (That was a far more pleasant experience for me than for my sister, Dolores, back in Chicago, having to open an envelope sent from a North Carolina funeral home. It took quite a bit of convincing to reassure her that it was just the bill for ambulance services and that I really *was* progressing.)

One day, one of the nurses approached my mother, asking to speak with her in private out in the hallway. With a sense of foreboding, she followed the nurse out of my room. Was I not getting better? Had something even worse than brain damage been discovered? What horrible thing could this "angel of mercy" want to discuss with her?

When they were safely out of earshot, the nurse turned to her and gently asked, "Is there something wrong with your daughter, ma'am?" (Something *wrong*? Of course, there was. I had been in a major auto accident, having only just survived it!)

"No", the nurse went on. "I mean, she's nineteen years old, ma'am, and she's *still* not married. Is there something wrong?" (Ah, the South...)

When I was discharged from the hospital at long last, we flew back to Chicago. (No more car, remember?) This was my first time on an airplane, and a memorable flight it was. The airline rules required that passengers be ambulatory—able to walk, be mobile or, in my case, be able to sit up. After lying in a hospital bed for all those weeks, just sitting up for any length of time was difficult, at best. Even the short taxi ride to the airport was a challenge. The motion of the vehicle, the surge of the oncoming traffic and the dizzying landscape whizzing by almost caused me to be carsick.

We boarded the aircraft, made our way down the aisle and found our seats. They were in the very last row of the plane, and the seatbacks wouldn't recline at all. As soon as we settled in, I knew I wouldn't be comfortable having to sit ramrod straight throughout the long flight ahead. The male flight attendant agreed to move us to seats that would recline, but we had to hurry because take-off was imminent. Without thinking, I just stood up, forgetting the overhead compartment was just inches above my head.

I was wearing a wig because I was still having a "bad hair day", or a "*no* hair day", I should say (still pretty bald after the brain surgery). But the wig was no cushion against the hard, molded ceiling of the overhead bin. I hit it with such force that the pain doubled me in half over the seatback in front of me. I was crying, my gauze eye patch for my double vision was soaked with tears, and I thought the flight attendant was going to faint, as well.

After all the drama subsided, our seats got changed, and the rest of the flight was uneventful. The flight attendant regained his composure and went about his duties offering gum to the passengers as he negotiated the narrow aisle.

"Chewin' gum? Chewin' gum? How's your little girl, ma'am? Chewin' gum?" (Oh, please, God. Let this end!)

ಚಿ☙ಐಜಿ⊷ಜಿ

Once back home, I still required regular, medical follow-up visits to monitor my healing progress. At one doctor's appointment, I sat among the other patients in the waiting room until it was my turn to be seen. After examining me, the doctor decided to give me a cortisone injection in the back of my neck to ease the pain that lingered from the whiplash injury. I screamed bloody murder the entire time it took to give me the injection, once again soaking my bandaged eye with tears. (Yep, I'm a crier.) When I left the examining room, there wasn't a soul there. (Who knew I could yell loudly enough to clear an entire waiting room?)

In the weeks that followed, I gradually regained my strength. Wearing special eyeglass lenses, my double vision was controlled finally and disappeared completely after about six months. (I still remember that the ophthalmologist had bad breath, particularly noticeable as he examined me and fitted my new glasses.) Frequently, my sister would come into my bedroom, armed with a yardstick so she could measure my hair growth. You might say that was her attempt at sibling levity to downplay my "tonsorial brevity".

I bought another car before going back to work and contacted the same auto insurance company to get coverage again. I filled out new paperwork, listing any accidents I "may have had". The serious young man across the desk from me bent his head over my completed application and quietly pored over my entries.

Suddenly, he looked up and said, "Oh! We studied about *you* in class. You were in the *'Don't'* column. Sorry, we can't insure you."

So, I had to scramble about, looking for another insurance company willing to take me on before I could drive my new car. (You see? The "Big Lie" continued to punish me.)

By the time I returned to work, I was still wearing my trusty wig. Weekly, a few of my co-workers would urge me to let them accompany me to the Ladies Room where I'd take off the wig so they could check on my hair "progress". You'd think they'd never seen a nearly bald woman before. Well, come to think of it, neither had I. (Hair grows one-half inch per month, by the way, in case anyone asks.)

Once back on the job, I found that I still had considerable difficulty with my short-term memory. What other people took for granted—learning new assignments or remembering everyday routines—slipped quickly from my memory's grasp. This was a residual effect of the brain injury. The man I worked for was very understanding, nevertheless. When he found that I had not completed certain daily tasks expected of me, he gently suggested that I maintain a notebook wherein I could add entries to help me remember the things I was supposed to accomplish during the day. (All well and good—that is, until I forgot where I put the notebook.)

Many people grow plants in an office setting, but I kept a small fishbowl on my file cabinet. It was home to a very pregnant guppy whose advancement I'd monitor daily. When I sensed that the births were imminent, I prepared a smaller glass bowl of water that I labeled "Maternity Ward" and placed it beside the larger one. (Guppies, themselves, are so small. What could you possibly call their offspring—"guppy puppies"?) At any rate, I knew to retrieve them as they were being born because I'd read that the fish ate their young after delivering.

My boss was in the midst of conducting a staff

meeting, and I was recording the meeting notes when mama started cranking out the newborn fishies. It's not that I wasn't expecting it. I just forgot to look up from my note taking. By the time I remembered, it was too late. I jumped up from my chair and raced toward the file cabinet just as she gulped down the last one.

I learned a valuable lesson from that experience, though. Sometimes you're the big fish, and sometimes you're the bait. It's all about survival in life, and sometimes you have to work hard and swim like hell just to save your own. Most of the effects of my brain injury regarding memory loss have vanished, I'm glad to say. With the passage of time, my memory is about as good as anyone's my age (except for forgetting the occasional watcha-ma-call-it or what's-his-name).

ᏣᎠᏟᏍᏓᏍᏃᏬ

P.S. My parents did forgive me for "the Big Lie". And even though the boyfriend was granted special leave from the Marine Corps to come visit me in the hospital, that didn't win him any bonus points with my folks.

- TWO -

Oh, No! Not *Again!*

How many people do you know who have been in *two* head-on collisions in their lifetimes and have lived to tell the tale? Yep, that's right. As if *one* weren't bad enough, less than three years later, that "invisible magnet", hidden somewhere in my car that seemed to draw other vehicles to me, activated itself again. But, my second head-on wasn't nearly as dramatic as the North Carolina accident, I'm happy to say.

I was driving one evening to my part-time job as a guitar teacher at a local music school. It had been raining most of the day, and even though the rain had stopped, the streets were still wet and slippery. As I waited to turn left into the parking lot across from the school, a car approaching from the opposite direction suddenly crossed the center line and veered into my driving lane.

The car struck mine head on, spinning me around

180° into the oncoming traffic. Like a metal ball in a pinball machine, my car careened wildly on the wet pavement and smashed into several cars before finally coming to a stop. (Game over.) What I remember next was being lifted into an ambulance and taken to the hospital. I recall hearing the whirring blades of a helicopter overhead and wondering if that meant I'd be on the evening news. I never did find out.

Interesting place, that ambulance. I say "place" because the interior of it looked like a miniature doctor's examining room (on wheels). And, the siren doesn't sound as loud *inside* the ambulance as it does from the outside (just in case you've ever wondered). In fact, according to a paramedic friend of mine, technology improvements over the years have reduced the inside-the-cab siren decibel level. Unfortunately, though, paramedics still suffer some hearing loss over time due to the daily assault on their eardrums, even with earplugs.

The good news for *me*, though, was that my injuries were much less severe than from my other head-on experience. The initial diagnosis indicated only a "sprained body" which sounds a lot worse than it actually turned out to be. The bad news was that my car was wrecked again, giving new meaning to the term "compact" car (although the body shop guy *was* able to put all of "Humpty Dumpty's" pieces back together again without any sign of damage).

☙❧⳼☙✦❧

About a year later, I got a job as a Government court reporter and was required to travel out of town with the administrative law judge for the hearings about every six weeks. The judge to whom I was assigned, a Jewish man, seemed always to disagree with me on every subject. If I'd say it's white, he'd say no, it's black. He had a short fuse, too, and frequently became exasperated with me, making any time I spent with him hard work.

We were sitting in a restaurant at dinner on our first night out on the road, and my mind began to wander as the judge droned on and on and on. I'm sure my eyes must have glazed over about the same time I stopped listening to his monologue (probably five or six paragraphs earlier). But, all of a sudden, I thought I heard him say something about "Jewish coffee". I knew I couldn't fake it to guess what the conversation had been about because I really hadn't been paying attention. So, I tentatively asked, "What *is* that?"

He responded in an impatient tone, "What is *what*?"

I said, "Well, I've heard of Irish coffee and Mexican coffee, but I don't know what 'Jewish' coffee is. What is it?" I asked again.

He exhaled slowly through his nose, looked me dead in the eye and replied in a measured tone, "I asked: '*Do you wish* coffee?'"

Well, my career as his court reporter certainly got off to a rocky start with that blunder. But, hey! It's an easy mistake anyone could have made. (I know this really doesn't have anything to do with topic of health, other than the fact that he really made me sick. But, it happened shortly after that second head-on auto collision, and it's always struck me funny, so I just wanted to share.)

CB ❧ CRSO ❦ ಬ

I've had a couple of *non*-motor mishaps that I can attribute to just plain carelessness on my part. When I was a kid, I managed to step barefoot on hot charcoal briquettes that someone had tossed *under* an unused picnic table at the lake so nobody would step on them. (Leave it to Beaver.)   Another time, I attempted to turn on a light switch that had its cover removed for repainting. I used a penny to try to flip the switch so I wouldn't get shocked if my finger accidentally touched it. *I* didn't get hurt, but the penny slipped and cut Abe Lincoln a new profile, blowing the nose right off his face when it made contact and sending a shock wave straight up my arm. (My hair is curly to this day.) But, other than the occasional fender bender in a parking lot or at a traffic light (never my fault, by the way...well, okay—maybe *once*), at least my automobile accident days had finally come to a halt. (I hope I didn't jinx myself just now by making that claim.)

I won't elaborate on the various sprains, cuts and bruises we all face while negotiating this occasionally perilous life, with or without an auto accident. But, I guess it would be appropriate at this point to reveal that I've also broken my arm twice, had surgery on both feet four times, knee surgery twice, carpal tunnel surgery on my wrists three times, breast cancer surgery twice and stitches to my head on three separate occasions after splitting it open (not counting the brain surgery).

Just like most people, I try to take care of my health as best I can, but you know what they say—"Split happens!"

- THREE -

My First Cruise...My First Gallbladder Attack

I went on my first cruise in 1978 on the Alaskan Inside Passage. Most people enjoy that type of cruise because the waters are always calm and the scenery, breathtaking. Leave it to me to be seasick the whole five days. At one point, I just wanted to go off and be by myself (the way animals do when they know it's "their time").

It was on one of those days when I just wanted solitude that I decided to take a walk around the open deck. The interior of the ship was bustling with activity and too many people in a hurry, it seemed. This was a vacation, I thought, so what's the rush? I wasn't in the mood for being around people who *were* enjoying themselves (since I wasn't), and I hoped the brisk air outside and some quiet time alone would take my mind off the queasy, unsettled feeling in my stomach that continued to plague me.

I pushed open the ship's heavy door, left the cozy warmth of the interior behind and stepped outside into the freezing cold. It was blustery on the open deck, and the cold air was intensified by the icy waters and glaciers all around us. Very soon, I began to shiver and looked for shelter from the stiff breeze biting my nose and cheeks.

I finally discovered a place in an alcove a few steps down and out of the wind. I stood there for a while, just trying to take deep breaths of air to overcome the persistent nausea, but that only seemed to make me feel worse. I waited there for a long time, it seemed, perspiration now collecting on my skin under all the layers of clothing I had on. That was a sure sign I'd be throwing up soon. (Feeling hot and cold at the same time—that's always my first warning signal. Stage 2 is coughing; Stage 3, get outta my way!)

As I stood there wondering just what people saw in cruising anyway, one of the ship's crewmen came by and asked me what was wrong. I told him I was extremely nauseated and was just standing there sheltered from the wind, trying to take in a few deep breaths.

He said, "Well, no *wonder* you're sick. I've been painting the deck all day and stored my paint cans beside where you're standing. You've been breathing in paint fumes. Go topside and take some deep breaths in the fresh air. Green is *not* your best color!"

I managed to get through the rest of the cruise and then spent a few days afterwards in California visiting family. But, the unsettled, churning feeling in my stomach stayed with me. I chalked it up to my cousin's pedal-to-the-metal driving on all those mountain turns as we went sightseeing in the wine country, remembering my lifelong tendency to get carsick. I returned home to Chicago a week later, still nauseated and still unable to get my "land legs".

❧❧❧❧❧❧

Trying to get my mind off of it, I took my mother out to dinner the next weekend. The restaurant, a favorite of ours, was famous for their roast duck dinners. That's something I don't often eat, and I was really looking forward to it despite my continued queasiness. Midway through the meal, though, I started to feel worse. Soon, a sharp, driving pain in my abdomen accompanied the nausea, forcing us to leave the restaurant even before finishing dinner. The server wrapped up both dinners to go (don't forget to throw in the dinner rolls!) and we headed toward home.

I felt too sick even to drive. I lay down on the back seat while my mother took the wheel. Halfway home, severe cramping and pain under my sternum suddenly engulfed me, rivaling the nausea. She had to pull off the road where I gave up what little of the duck dinner I had eaten. By the time we got home, I was unable to breathe without the pain knifing straight through me.

(Don't you hate people who telephone a hospital to describe symptoms and then expect a magic cure over the phone? That was me.) Of course, I was told to come to the Emergency Room to be examined, so we got back into the car and headed for the hospital. After the physical exam, several x-rays and an ultrasound, it was confirmed: I'd had a major gallbladder attack and would require surgery to remove it.

The nausea and pain I was experiencing throughout

the cruise and the week that followed were minor "warning" attacks and not seasickness, after all. It was probably a good thing that the major attack happened at home when it did. Had it occurred on board the ship in Alaska, the next paragraph of this book might have detailed what it's like to be airlifted by helicopter from a cruise ship to a hospital for treatment.

But, here was the kicker—the doctor said I'd have to begin a special low-fat diet to prepare my body for the surgery that would be scheduled *six* weeks later! I never did get to finish that roast duck dinner. My mother put it in my refrigerator before taking me to the Emergency Room that night. She stayed overnight at my home, came back to the hospital the next day and polished it off herself later that night after visiting hours ended.

♋ ✦ ♋ ♒ ✦ ♒

The six weeks passed finally (*unlike* the gallstone), and I had the surgery, during which the doctor removed *one* gallstone. All that pain and all I had to show for it was one stone. It was a big one, though, about the size (and color, by the way) of a macadamia nut. It sat there in a jar of formaldehyde on my bedside table in the hospital room, staring at me with its pale golden eye. I watched it, too, wondering what I might do with this souvenir once I got home.

When I was discharged, I took the gallstone home with me in its jar, and each day I continued to look at it, sitting there in its watery prison. I wondered what it felt like. I wondered how much it weighed. I wondered until I couldn't stand not knowing. So, I carefully opened the container, took a spoon to lift it out (I couldn't touch it yet—*yuck!*) and hoped the air wouldn't make it disintegrate instantly like the taped message at the beginning of each episode of "Mission Impossible". Then I touched it. Exactly like a macadamia nut! I got a paring knife, poked at it and finally decided to cut it in half, wondering what the inside of a gallstone looked like. More macadamia nut!

That's when I got a brainstorm. This was my trophy, and I would wear it proudly for all to see, a reminder of the agony and suffering I had endured all those weeks. (I can be so dramatic at times.) I took a gold neck chain (this happened in the days before gold got expensive) and a bottle of Elmer's Glue. I cemented together the two halves of the gallstone, sandwiching the gold chain in between. A coat of clear nail polish over the stone completed the creation. This was my prize, my $2,500.00 necklace, compliments of Blue Cross/Blue Shield. Wear it proudly! (I still do, now and then.)

ॐ ॐ ॐ ॐ ॐ

I healed eventually and went back to the tradition of taking my mom out to dinner every Sunday night. While we were seated in a restaurant one evening, I spotted an older woman across the dining room slowly leading an even older woman by the arm to their table.

Wanting to compliment my own mother who was in her early seventies by then, I said, "Look. That's you and me in twenty-five years."

She leaned over and tactfully whispered, "Which one am I?" (A good sense of humor runs in the family.)

- FOUR -

Rating Your Health Care Facility

Everyone uses an individual, personalized system for assessing the quality of a hospital. Some people are very methodical, doing Internet searches to uncover patient complaints, securing word-of-mouth testimonials from family and friends, and ensuring, in general, that their ultimate choice is a safe place to receive care. Others rate hospital effectiveness by the kind of attention and hands-on treatment they've experienced personally. Still others consider the proximity to home as the deciding factor when choosing a hospital. As most doctors (in larger cities) maintain offices adjacent to a hospital, it's somewhat important to find a facility nearby for convenience sake, especially if you anticipate several follow-up visits.

There are two hospitals close to where I live now, one within walking distance, in fact. I prefer that one since it's easier for me to walk there (now) for follow-up care than to drive around and around in search of a parking place. Plus, it's good exercise. The sister hospital is about seven miles away but has no Emergency Room (high on my "must have" list, as you may have surmised). One of my surgeons considered this important, too, but for a contrasting reason. Without an Emergency Room attached to the facility, there would be no chance of him getting "bumped" from a surgery slot in favor of an incoming, emergency surgical case. ("Time is money, boys and girls!")

I personally use an even more down-to-earth gauge of patient satisfaction: the quality of the socks and the quality of the food. This might seem a bit unconventional but, normally, first impressions will give an indicator of what lies ahead.

At every admission, you are issued a regulation won't-stay-closed hospital gown and a pair of ugly socks. (Leave your fuzzy, pink slippers at home, Matilda!) The gowns are usually a blue and white cotton job of varying pattern, with long, narrow ties at the back of the neck to keep it closed. Sometimes, these gowns have snaps on the sleeves, too, so that the arms and torso can be accessed easily, if required. A couple longer ties are sewn in at one hipline and at the edge in the back of the gown. Presumably, these are sufficient to hold the gown closed, but we all know better. (Where do you suppose the term, "ICU", came from?) With only minor deviation, every hospital I've ever been in has furnished essentially the same type of gown to its patients.

The slipper socks, however, are the signature element that makes every health care facility unique. Here's a brief description of many of the slipper socks available, according to "quality" level:

o cheap, blue, foam rubber slip-ons (which began to disintegrate even before I was discharged from the hospital);

o thin, white, cotton socks with little powder-blue paw-print treads on the bottom, complete with puff paint "claws" (but useless for re-wear at home because they don't last very long);

o medium-density cocoa-colored cotton (how alliterative!) with white, striped treads (lasts a little bit longer); and

o heavyweight powder-blue cotton jobs with dark-blue leather, diamond-shaped treads on the underside (very pricey-looking but too thick for re-wear at home during the summer).

"You get what you pay for", I suppose. Or, maybe I should say, "You *pay* for what you get". The blue-sock hospital, located about thirty miles from my home, even charged for parking next door—*and* wouldn't validate!

C3 ꙮ C3 80 ꙮ 80

While we're on the subject of ratings, a word of caution: do *not* judge the quality of physicians by their handwriting. My guess is that they took so many handwritten notes while in med school that it ruined their penmanship for life. So, that's why I normally cut them some slack in that area. In fact, I might even be a little suspicious if I ever found a doctor with *good* handwriting.

I'm sure that's one of the main reasons doctors dictate their progress notes into a tape recorder for transcription later. Otherwise, there would be any number of chances for error if a clerical actually had to transcribe from handwritten notes. (A classic example of this occurred the time my dad received a filled prescription for something to help him with *morning sickness*.)

Although practically indecipherable, it's funny how doctors' scribbles appear so similar to one another's, nevertheless. (I feel the same way about graffiti. To my untrained eye, all graffiti appears to have been created by the same gang artist, no matter where in the world you see it.) Just imagine what your insides might look like if a surgeon's penmanship were any indicator of his surgical skill.

ය‍&‍ය‍&‍ම‍&‍ම

As to the dreaded topic of hospital food, I really don't think I've ever had a bad meal in a hospital, or maybe it's just that I'm not that picky. If I don't have to prepare it and do the dishes afterwards, then whatever I'm fed is fine with me, especially if someone else is doing the serving and the cleaning up.

At one hospital in Chicago, I was able to order lobster and actually had wine with each dinner. The place could have passed itself off as a fine dining establishment (except for the blood draw and the bedpan part.) At another hospital, I was permitted, even encouraged, to go to their kitchen myself to get my own munchies. (I guess they were getting tired of me hitting that call button for snack service the ten days I was there.) Breakfast, lunch and dinner were still brought in by trolley at the appointed times, of course. The last hospital I was in required you to dial a telephone extension and place your food orders for the entire day by phone—just like calling for take-out, but without having to tip the delivery guy.

Sometimes, food can be brought in from outside

sources, with or without the hospital's knowledge. I had the first chilidog of my life while at the hospital in Roanoke, Virginia. I had gotten into a conversation with one of the hospital orderlies and told him I had never heard of a chilidog, much less eaten one, and he offered to go out and buy one for me. I'm hooked on chilidogs to this day.

While in a hospital another time, I made friends with two lab technicians during my stay. One of them, a guy with a big, toothy grin that looked like a row of Chicklets, was sweet on me and overheard the other tech offering to sneak in a pizza for us during his night shift. I was all for it, and we were happily enjoying our late-night snack when "Smiley" breezed into my room, carrying his *own* pizza. When he saw the open box revealing our half-eaten pizza, his big smile faded faster than a pair of red socks washed in hot water. So, to break the awkward silence and to be polite, I had to share his, too. (It was a long time before I could even *look* at a pizza again after that night.)

But, there's more to the story. "Chicklet Boy" just couldn't take the hint and continued to bring me little treats and small gifts for the rest of my hospital stay, even though I discouraged it. Had I not been discharged, I might have needed a restraining order to keep him at bay. (Remember, it takes only one small letter to change the word "talking" to "stalking".)

◌ↄ ♥ ◌ↄ ಔ ↄ ♥ ಔ

Now, hospital patients are a whole other matter. These are your neighbors for a while and, like neighbors or relatives, you just can't pick 'em. A hospital I was in many years ago required that you share the bathroom with the patient in the next room. (Each patient's room was separated by connecting doors to the bathroom.) This was back in the days when even having a television in your room wasn't a "given" but had to be rented if you wanted entertainment during your stay.

Normally, I get on quite well with hospital roommates (and neighbors), but this particular time there was a sticking point that prevented any camaraderie. The man in the next room had a TV, and I did not. I tried every tactic I could think of to engineer an invitation to his room to watch TV with him after visiting hours ended. But, no soap. I was especially bummed because I was missing one of my favorite programs at the time—"Bonanza", that old-time Western classic.

So, I fixed him. If I couldn't watch, at least I'd make sure he didn't enjoy his evening either. I had overheard the nurse telling him he had to have an enema, so I did what any resentful person would do: I locked the bathroom door from my side. I'm sorry about that now, but at the time, vengeance was mine, and it sure felt good. That entire scene could have been avoided had he shared (or had I not been too cheap to rent my own TV in the first place).

CB⇄CBꚘ⤳Ꚙ

At the risk of being thought of as totally superficial, I should point out that there's one legitimate indicator of hospital quality that I value highly—diagnostic accuracy. As part of the pre-op testing before surgery, patients over the age of thirty-five have to have an EKG taken. My test results indicated "borderline EKG", which I found out later means exactly what you think it means. At that point, the radiologist makes the recommendation to the surgical team as to whether or not it's in your best interests to proceed. (In my case, they proceeded. I guess I was on the right side of the "border".)

About eight months later, I had to have surgery again but at a different hospital and using a different surgeon. Another EKG. I didn't see the results of that one, however, until *after* my surgery. Imagine my shock after I read the words "possible septal infarct" on the EKG report. That means *heart attack*, people! I almost had a heart attack on the spot after reading that report. At my follow-up visit to the surgeon's office, I questioned him about the comment on the EKG.

He said, "Well, you lived, didn't you? Sometimes EKG's give false readings." (Case closed.)

I wasn't satisfied, though, and pursued the matter. I got an appointment with a cardiologist and presented both EKG reports to him to interpret. He ran four more EKG's there in his office, and they all indicated "within normal limits". The cardiologist said he suspected that the placement of the leads by the technician at the other hospital hadn't been quite where they should have been, and that's what caused the false reading of "possible septal infarct." (Whew! I get to live to enjoy another sunset!)

଼ ☙ ଼ ☙ ଼

One weekend, I was trimming hedges in my back yard and got distracted. (Always pay attention when you're holding an electric hedge trimmer!) Well, you can see what's coming. In my haste to finish the job, I sliced a notch in the second joint of my forefinger and tried to "fix it" myself. I made several failed attempts to stop the bleeding by pressing a plastic baggie of ice cubes against my paper towel-wrapped finger.

I finally resigned myself into going to the Emergency Room for treatment. After sitting an interminable amount of time in the waiting room with my hand poised in the air as if I were trying to stop traffic, I finally got to see the E.R. doctor.

He took one look at it and said, "I can't give you stitches now because you've waited too long. This will leave a permanent scar." (I felt like saying, "Does this include the inordinate amount of time I've been sitting here, waiting to see you?")

Well, I was determined to prove him wrong. Once the wound healed, I massaged it with Vitamin E cream every chance I got. Each time I thought about it, I'd work the skin to flatten it, sometimes just pressing my thumb against it as I went about my day. You can't even see the scar today. So, persistence does pay off.

Speaking of thumbs, I once worked at an office where periodically, we'd play a game called "What Good Are Your Thumbs?" Whoever came up with the most uses for thumbs was the winner (of nothing). We had a list of answers like: You need your thumb for hitchhiking, for being an umpire at a baseball game ("Yerrrrr out!"), for shaking hands, for snapping your fingers and for easing your swimsuit bottom out of your butt (something only women could understand). Now, I can add to the list, pressing down a scar until it disappears.

ॐ᠅ॐ᠅ॐ

I took a cruise vacation to the continent of Antarctica one year. The ship, with its icebreaking capability, edged as close to land as possible, but then a motorized, inflatable raft was lowered into the water from the side of the ship, transporting fifteen people at a time closer to shore. Dressed in a bulky down-filled parka over clothing and wearing rubber boots up to the knee, you'd have to swing your legs over the side of the rubber raft and ease yourself into the almost knee-deep, icy-cold water. Each of us in our outsized gear felt we looked much like the Abominable Snowman as we waded and waddled the last few feet to shore. Once on land, we were permitted to explore on our own, and only a few areas were off limits to tourists.

One of the places we visited in Antarctica was a research station that you could walk to from the raft landing point. It was almost a mile walk over a gravely road (which is not as much fun as you'd think, plodding along in the oversized parka and rubber boots). I began my self-guided tour of the research station and wandered into the dining hall, then the library and finally, the meager lounge. The unoccupied room housed nothing more than a few stools and a guitar propped against the bar.

The lounge had a quaint charm all its own, though, and I wanted to secure a higher vantage point for a better view to photograph it. Still wearing my parka and ungainly rubber boots, I perched on one of the barstools and then attempted to stand up while trying to balance my heels on its rungs. In a split second, the barstool tipped, I tipped with it and crashed into the guitar next to it, causing a deafening *T-W-A-N-G!!!* (but no real melody you'd recognize).

When I landed, my head hit the bar hard and split open at the base of my skull. I just sat there on the floor until I stopped seeing stars. (Speaking of stars, did you know you that the Big Dipper appears upside *down* in the southern hemisphere? Of course, another constellation, the Southern Cross, can't even be seen from the northern hemisphere.) But, I digress.

I picked myself and the guitar up and went in search of medical attention. I spotted someone working in the library, so I went in and asked to see a doctor. The research station, one of many in Antarctica, was inhabited year round by twelve men from Poland, but none of them spoke more than a smattering of English.

"Doctor, no tours", I was told.

Without speaking, I just wiped the back of my head with my hand and presented it palm up, which convinced the attendant to find the doctor quickly due to the amount of blood he saw which was now running down my back.

Everyone does double-duty at these research stations, sometimes even triple-duty, as was the case with my doctor/taxi driver/mechanic. He wore blue jeans, a lumberjack shirt and a plaid, cloth headband to hold his shoulder-length hair in place. He motioned to me to follow him into his sparsely-furnished office. Giving a cursory glance around, I noticed a few tools of his trade casually lying about on a side table next to jars, bottles and a spit basin. (I wondered how you'd ask "Are those sterilized?" in Polish but knew I probably wouldn't be understood.)

The doctor examined me in silence and, except for the only three words of English he uttered, he never spoke another word. When he was ready to close the wound with stitches (without using anything to numb the area first), all he said was: "This will hurt." (Yikes! I understood *that*.)

When he finished suturing, I thanked him and took out my wallet to pay him. But, he shook his head and just pointed to my camera and then to me.

Sure, I'd love to have someone there take our picture. This appeared to please him even though he didn't seem to want the photo for himself. Oh, well, *I* did. That would be quite a keepsake.

Another researcher was summoned to take the photo, and then my doctor "put on his other hat" and drove me back to our landing point in his taxi. (Too bad I didn't need an oil change, too. Then I'd be "three for three"!) People out working along the way stopped what they were doing and just stared as we drove past on the bumpy road. Later on, I learned that the taxi is used only when transporting dignitaries. (Who *was* she?)

By the time we got back to the landing point, news of my accident had gotten embellished along the way and spread among my fellow tourists like a bad rash.

"You were so lucky to need only a few stitches", one of them said to me. "We heard you fell from the lighthouse!"

We returned to the cruise ship, and once on board, I sought out the ship's doctor who assured me that I had received fine medical care at the research station. After acknowledging his instructions to have the stitches removed once I reached home, I went back to my cabin to rest. I ordered room service for my lunch, telling the cabin steward that whatever they were serving everyone else in the dining room would be just fine.

After a short time, there was a knock at my door, and I opened it to find the cabin steward standing there with my tray. I showed him in and watched as he carefully set it down on the table. Ceremoniously, he lifted the metal cover off the plate and presented my lunch to me with a slight bow. Meatloaf. How sad!   There's just no way to put a positive spin on that one.

CR➤CR₧➤₧₧

Here's one final observation while we're on the subject of health care facilities. When you go for an MRI (magnetic resonance imaging), you must remove whatever metal objects you're wearing (wristwatch, rings, bra with metal hooks, etc.) before getting into the MRI "tunnel" and deposit them into a gym locker. I was dressing afterwards but didn't realize I had forgotten to retrieve my wristwatch from the locker before leaving the place. I didn't notice it was missing until I reached my office, some twenty miles away.

When I telephoned the MRI facility, I was told they had discovered it already and said I could pick it up after work. I responded that I wouldn't be able to get there before they closed. So, the technician told me she would just take my watch over to the drug store down the street on her lunch hour, and I could pick it up there after work. When I arrived there that evening, my wristwatch was waiting for me in an envelope at the pharmacy. Now, *that's* customer service!

– FIVE –

Insurance: The "Titanic" of All Challenges

As if being sick or injured weren't enough to deal with, you have the pursuit of life, liberty and insurance reimbursement to look forward to, assuming you're among those lucky enough to afford medical insurance in the first place. Fortunately for me, I had two medical insurance policies, up until I lost my last job, that is.

Over the years, I had maintained the one I signed up for initially at my first job with the Federal Government when I was seventeen years old. (That was so long ago that I think the premium amount for it may have been written originally in Roman numerals.) When I left the Federal service over twenty-six years later, I continued to pay the premiums on that policy because the couple of jobs I had after that didn't offer health insurance.

Finally, I landed a job with a larger company which did extend medical insurance to its employees, and I enrolled in the plan but decided to retain the other one, as well. So, my old standby policy became my "secondary", as it's called in the insurance game, and my work policy became my "primary" insurance. Now, the fun begins.

My primary coverage (let's call that "Policy A") required that I use a "preferred provider"—a vendor on their "A" list, so to speak—in order to get reimbursed for medical expenses. That's a reasonable request, but sometimes you have no control over which provider or vendor is actually used. Here's an example.

I had to have some lab tests at the hospital a few months after a surgery I had undergone. Imagine my surprise when the insurance "Explanation of Benefits" notice arrived in the mail, showing that they had paid *nothing* because I didn't use a preferred provider. I'm not one to accept things without question, though, so I telephoned for more information. I asked why the charge for lab work wasn't reimbursed when I had no control over which lab the hospital used. I was asked the name and address of the hospital, and when I told them, I was informed that they would now pay the benefit. Since the hospital is a preferred provider (or "*in* network", as they termed it), they would extend that status to the non-preferred lab, as well.

But, you see? You have to fight for these things, and sometimes it takes several phone calls to resolve an issue.

ॐ☙❧ॐ

Speaking of fights, I battled with the insurance company for some eighteen months after a particular charge was incurred. Here's the story. After having knee surgery, a walker was ordered by the surgeon and was delivered to my hospital room the day I was discharged. The invoice accompanying the walker listed the name of the company to whom I should remit payment. (Let's call them "Provider 1".) However, the amount due was shown on the invoice as $0.00. I assumed this meant that they would bill my insurance company first and that nothing was due from me at present.

About a month later, I received notice from my "Policy A" insurance (my policy from work) indicating that the entire amount of the bill was being put towards my annual deductible which I had not yet met for the year. Therefore, there was nothing left over to pay "Provider 1". No one contacted me further, so I just assumed that "Provider 1" had received the same notice. "Provider 1" would then bill "Policy B" (my secondary insurance), which is the normal flow of events when two insurance policies are involved. Confused yet? Wait. It gets better.

A full year later, I got a bill in the mail from "Provider 2" (whose name was shown in tiny letters on the original invoice, listing themselves as *primary payer*). Believe me, I was as puzzled then as you probably are now. I telephoned "Provider 2" and questioned why they hadn't billed my secondary insurance, "Policy B", instead of billing me.

I was told, "We don't do that."

They wanted their money *now* (twelve months after I had been issued the walker). I was advised to file my own claim for reimbursement with "Policy B", after first paying "Provider 2" for the walker. Sensing I had nothing to gain by protesting, I paid "Provider 2", mailed in my claim form and proof of payment to "Policy B" and waited once again for the reimbursement check to arrive.

A month later, an "Explanation of Benefits" notice from "Policy B" came in the mail, showing nothing would be paid because I had used a nonpreferred provider. (Here we go again!) I picked up the telephone and called them to point out their error. I had checked my policy benefits book and saw that "Provider 1" was indeed a preferred provider, and I reminded them that it was "Provider 1" who had sent me the original invoice. So, the insurance representative changed the provider's name on my claim form, and I was assured that the benefit check would now be issued. Well, it was issued, all right—to *Provider 1*, rather than to me!

So, now I'm mad. I called the "Policy B" insurance company back to point out that the check should have been paid to me and not to the provider since *I'm* the one who had paid the bill. I was told they would look into it and would call me back.

A couple weeks went by and I hadn't heard anything, so I called the insurance company again. This time my call was transferred to an unsympathetic, stick-up-her-butt insurance representative. She coolly advised me that their records showed it was actually "Provider 2" who delivered the walker to my hospital room, and *that* was the controlling factor, not whose name was on the invoice. They had incorrectly paid "Provider 1", after all.

Furthermore, she said that since "Provider 2" was a nonpreferred provider, nothing would be paid to them either. She instructed me to contact "Provider 1" to have them return the erroneous payment to the insurance company. (At that point, I think I said something like "I'm not going to do your job, too". Then, I believe, I hung up on her.)

Back on the telephone again after I had taken the weekend to calm down, I called "Provider 1" to ask for their help. The "Provider 1" medical equipment rep assured me that they were, indeed, the provider. They subcontract out to "Provider 2" because they ("Provider 1") don't furnish the required medical equipment in my area. She gave me the name and address of an appeals board and advised me to pursue my claim through them. Even the rep said it would be futile to deal with "The Ice Queen" again (the nickname for the Policy 2 representative that we both agreed on), admitting that she, too, had been unsuccessful in past dealings with her.

A few days later, I opened my mail box to find a heavy envelope sent to me by "The Ice Queen". It was a copy of my thick insurance policy benefits book with two pages highlighted—both of them indicating that my policy pays *only* if I use preferred providers. (Well, duh!) She had spent $2.11 in postage to mail me something I already knew. So much for saving the insurance company money. (By this time, if I thought she was a pain in the neck *before* the packet arrived, I now had a *lower* opinion of her, if you get my meaning.)

To add insult to injury, so to speak, I used the walker only twice: once to get from the car into the house the day I returned from the hospital and later that night when I went to the bathroom. That walker has never been used since except by my friend, Nancy, who borrowed it to use as a joke at a retirement party she attended.

I took the medical equipment rep's advice and sat down to compose my letter to the insurance appeals board, playing out the scenario as I have here. Within two weeks, I received a decision letter, agreeing that "Provider 1" had, indeed, supplied me with the walker, and that I should expect a reimbursement check directly from "Provider 1" (*not* the insurance company) within four to six weeks. Two months later, the reimbursement check finally arrived in the mail. Whew!

It's no wonder that, generally speaking, people feel as if they're adrift in a sea of hopelessness when it comes to insurance. But, if you learn nothing else from my saga, just remember these three little words: Persist! Persist! Persist!

CB&CREO&EO

During the eighteen months following multiple hospital admissions, I received so many bills from so many providers that I actually had to create a computer spreadsheet just to keep track of who charged what, who paid what, and who's on first. I had mentioned to one of my favorite doctors that he was charging much less than all the other doctors I was seeing and commented that he should consider boosting his fees to keep up with the medical crowd. He laughed it off but did take the spreadsheet from me to "study".

Long story short, the next bill he sent me was for $200.00 instead of the customary $75.00 he had been charging me in the past for office visits! Fortunately, I still paid only the $15.00 co-payment as I did before because of my insurance coverage. But, I wondered how much of the information I had shared with him influenced his new billing.

And even that bill was cause for some head shaking. At the top of the invoice in block letters appeared the following: *IF PAYING BY MASTERCARD OR VISA, FILL OUT BELOW.* Then, a space appeared for the credit card number, its expiration date, a signature line and the amount to be paid. Following that was a detailed description of the medical services rendered.

Now, get this—at the bottom of the invoice was this *important message regarding your account. Please note that this practice does not accept payment by credit card. Please remit your payment by check or money order. Thank you.* (Huh?)

CB 🦢 CRFD 🐦 ƏD

In the interest of balance, there's one insurance carrier that *does* get extremely high marks from me— its logo is the famous duck in the TV commercials that loudly proclaims its name (and it rhymes with "*Baflac*"). I secured this insurance coverage through my employer a few years ago to help pay the bills when I became sidelined with illness or injury. At the time, I contemplated signing up for only the personal accident expense policy (given my track record). But the insurance representative who came to our office encouraged me to consider taking the cancer plan, as well, because of my family history (both my mother and her father died of cancer).

Despite this history, I honestly believed I'd never use the cancer policy. Still, something told me to purchase it. Perhaps I thought it might increase my chances of warding off cancer if I did, like a lucky charm. It's the old "apple-a-day-keeps-the-doctor-away" adage—you eat the apple, partly out of blind obedience to the maxim you've heard all your life and partly because you're pretty sure it *will* help and don't want to take the chance that it won't. So, I bought the policy.

Just four years later I *was* diagnosed with cancer

and was so grateful I'd signed up for that policy, too. It helped so much to have a caring, thorough insurance representative during that difficult time to assist me with my all my claim filing. He'd call me from time to time just to see how I was doing (even saying he prayed for me during the months I underwent treatment). It goes without saying that you have enough on your mind just dealing with injury or illness, the seemingly endless stream of doctor and hospital visits and bills, the delayed payments by insurance companies to these providers, and the pain and suffering of the body just trying to heal. How comforting it was to feel I now had someone from the wacky world of medical insurance in my corner, someone who'd help me receive all the benefits I was entitled to from those policies.

During the years that I've maintained the accident and cancer policies, I've been reimbursed almost *ten* times the amount I've paid for them in annual premiums. (This reads like a commercial endorsement, doesn't it?) Sure, I'd had a couple unusual years of multiple injuries, illnesses and claims which resulted in all those benefit payments. But, even so, I certainly have gotten the mileage out of that insurance coverage! (*Your* mileage may vary.)

C3 ও C3 ৪০ ও ৪০

There was the tale of a doctor who died and went to Heaven, but he was stopped at the Pearly Gates by St. Peter who asked why he should be let in.

The physician replied, "Well, I've been a doctor my entire professional life, mending broken bones and healing illnesses. I've been compassionate with my patients, fair in my billing and always honest in my dealings with people."

"All right, fair enough", St. Peter said, and let him into Heaven.

Awhile later, a nurse died and went to Heaven. Again, St. Peter stopped her at the Pearly Gates and asked her to tell him why she should be allowed in.

The nurse responded, "I've been a nurse my whole career. I've sat with patients when they got good news and bad. I've assisted doctors, tried always to be compassionate with patients and cheerful when they needed cheering up."

"Okay, already. You're good. C'mon in", said St. Peter.

Then, an HMO Administrator died and went to Heaven. St. Peter stopped him in his tracks and said, "You can't come into Heaven unless you convince me why I should let you in.

The HMO Administrator sniffed, "Why, St. Peter. I'm an HMO Administrator. *That's* why."

St. Peter just responded, "Okay, okay. Come in. But you can stay only three days."

– SIX –

Teaching the Teacher

A valuable skill I've learned to develop over the years is how to bandage myself using my non-dominant hand. I guess this hails back to my grammar school days when I got plenty of practice at it while caring for a broken arm—twice.

I broke my right arm the first time after falling off the stone pedestal of a birdbath in my back yard during the summertime. My dad had taken the top part off to repaint it, and the base was just too attractive for kids to resist, in fact perfect for playing "statue" with a neighborhood friend. I climbed up onto the pedestal, became the statue and struck a pose. She was the drunk who staggered into the gallery, knocking the statue off the pedestal. (I know. We were idiots. I can't even imagine how the rest of the scenario was supposed to play out.)

A year and a half later, I broke the same arm while playing jump rope during recess on an icy, snow-covered school playground in wintry Chicago. (The cold weather must freeze the common sense portion of the brain.) Being experienced in the area of fractures, I recognized immediately that my arm was broken (looked broken, felt broken, *must* be broken).

I walked up the steps to the convent to find someone to call my mother to take me to the hospital. I rang the bell with my "good" hand and then resumed cradling my injured wing. A nun answered the door, and her eyes opened wide when she saw the unnatural direction my hand was taking.

She invited me inside to the warmth of the entry hall and paled as I told her what had happened—a literal vision in black and "white". She wheeled around and headed toward what turned out to be a liquor cabinet, offering me a drink to calm me (?) down while I waited patiently.

When I said, "No, thank you, just call my mom, please" (I was only in the 6th grade, for crying out loud!), she downed the shot glass of brown liquid, herself, and then reached for the telephone.

Once the plaster cast was removed from my arm a few weeks later, I became quite adept at applying an Ace bandage wrap to support my arm as it continued to heal. For a short time, I even convinced my teacher that the doctor permitted *only* crayon coloring and no actual writing with that hand until the arm healed completely. (I continued to be an idiot.)

ෆ෨ඟ෨෫෨෬

One winter day during the 1970's, I broke my ankle while snow skiing (again, with the snow). I remember that the Ski Patrol guys were called and put me on a stretcher behind their sled. Then, one of them lay on top of me as we glided down to the first aid station there at the ski resort. (Straps would have done just fine, thank you. Jocks!)

At the first aid station, I wouldn't permit the nurse to cut off the leg of my brand-new ski pants, so they just put me in a temporary leg splint *over* the pants. By that time, it was too swollen for a plaster cast anyway, so I was instructed to see my own doctor the next day to have the ankle casted.

My friends drove me home and carried me up the stairs to the front door. My sister answered the doorbell and gave me that "Mom-and-Dad-are-going-to-kill-you-when-they-get-home" look but immediately came to my aid. My friends left, and Dolores helped me sit down on an ottoman next to a living room chair. Then, she proceeded to wheel me toward the bathroom on the ottoman where I could change out of my clothes.

With her hands on my shoulders and my bandaged leg poised straight out in front of me like a battering ram, she yelled "Charge!" and propelled me forward through the house. Skillfully, she navigated past walls, the dining room table and chairs, and we reached the bathroom safely at last. I sat down on the toilet seat lid while she gently lifted my foot up and onto the small footstool we kept beside it.

She eased me out of my new ski pants, assuring me she'd be able to re-wrap me without any difficulty, saying "I know what I'm doing."

She began working purposefully and methodically, wrapping what seemed like miles of Ace bandage around and around my broken ankle and up my leg. She was definitely "all business", a determined look on her young face as she bandaged in silence, her arms flying. When she finished, she clapped her hands as if to dust them off and then reached to help me up. But, when I tried to stand, I found she had bandaged me to the footstool! We both needed a light moment by that time and had a good laugh over it, that is, until Mom and Dad got home.

My leg stayed in a cast from my toes to my knee for six weeks and, obviously, during that time, the hair on my leg continued to grow and then began to itch. They say never insert anything into the cast, and there's a good reason for that. I took a slender, metal, letter opener, tried to poke it down into the cast to ease the itching, and wouldn't you know it? I lost it. It just dropped straight down into the cast and got hopelessly lodged there. Frequently, I'd try to lift my leg up into the air to try to shake out the letter opener, but it was in there for good.

Finally, at the end of six weeks, it was time to remove the plaster cast. I asked the doctor to be careful and try to get it off in one piece because I had plans for it. Expertly, he guided the electric saw up the length of the cast, knowing just how much pressure to put on the saw blade (thankfully). He slowly eased the cast off my leg, and as he did, the letter opener clanked onto the floor. Once it was removed, the cast snapped back together again like a spring-loaded clam shell, the seam barely visible.

I brought the cast home with me, painted it a neon color (in vogue at the time), stuck it upright in a shoe by the front door and made an umbrella stand out of it. Another trophy I planned to keep forever! (I sold it at a garage sale the next summer.)

ॐ❧ CRED ❧ ॐ

During the 1980's, I had foot surgery eight times in all, four for each foot. Once again, I had to learn to change my own bandages between doctor's visits. Having had surgery on both feet simultaneously the first time around, I developed a unique and "attractive" way to secure the bandages to give both support and comfort. The doctor even called it "ingenious" and asked me to show him my technique so he could use it on other patients.

During another period of recovery, I demonstrated to a physical therapist a way I had devised of folding together and then cutting multiple adhesive strips at the same time instead each one individually. Not only did it save time, but it ensured perfectly uniform lengths for all of the strips for bandaging. (See? I'm just not another pretty face!)

The casual observer just might sweep all of this into the category of "Get a life", but I'm a big fan of developing alternative skills. I mean, you just never know.

CB ❦ CRED ❦ ED

I had surgery to repair a torn meniscus (knee cartilage) suffered from a bad fall I took from a ladder. Neither I, nor the surgeon's patient care coordinator, remembered to get "pre-authorization" from the insurance company before having the procedure, however. The penalty for this lapse on our part was that the insurance company reimbursed only ten per cent of the doctor's bill. I appealed their decision, and submitted a letter signed by the surgeon as part of the evidence to support my claim. It described in detail why the procedure was "medically necessary" (an insurance buzz word) and requested that they reconsider their previous decision to deny payment of ninety per cent of his charges.

(Well, *he* didn't actually write the letter. *I* did.) His patient care coordinator telephoned me one day and told me in confidence that she hated writing letters, wasn't any good at it and didn't even know how to begin this one. (This was a woman whose former career before working for the surgeon involved selling ladies swimsuits.) She asked if I would write the letter for her if she fed me the pertinent details. Since I've always been fond of writing, I told her I would.

The finished product was a two-pager, and according to her, it covered with total clarity every single point she wanted to make, including insertion of all of the appropriate medical jargon. She said she never would have been able to construct it as well as I did, and the insurance company was certain to reconsider their denial after reading it.

Well, they did reconsider it, and then they denied it again for the same reason—no pre-authorization for the surgery. It didn't turn out all badly, though. Fortunately, I still had my trusty secondary insurance. I submitted the claim to them, and they picked up the tab for the unpaid ninety per cent of the bill, despite the absence of pre-authorization, which their plan required also. (God bless oversight!) So, all things considered, it was an elaborate exercise, but "all's well that end's well".

ॐ ☙ ॐ ☙

On the morning before I was to leave on an adventure vacation to Mongolia, the Gobi Desert and Siberia, I went out to the garden to water my plants. I balanced on one of the rustic railroad ties that framed the flowerbeds so I wouldn't get my shoes wet on the grass. Trying to detangle the garden hose, I lost my footing, slipped on the wet timber and hit the wooden fence hard, cutting my forehead open right at the hairline. I tried in vain to get the bleeding to stop but finally resigned myself into going to the hospital Emergency Room for treatment.

I fashioned an icepack out of paper towels wrapped around ice cubes. At each stoplight, I'd open the car door to wring out the melting ice in the paper towels, leaving a trail of blood all the way to the hospital (like a macabre version of the *"Hansel and Gretel"* and the bread crumbs fairy tale).

At the front desk, I removed the soggy paper towels that held what few ice cubes remained and revealed my head wound. I was asked if I had a doctor on staff.

"Only a gynecologist," I replied. "But, I need someone to look at the *other* end."

I had to get stitches, and the doctor in the Emergency Room instructed me to return in ten days to have them removed. I explained that I was leaving on vacation the next day and would be in a very rural area. He told me to go to a doctor there to have the stitches removed. I repeated that the area would be *very* rural with no medical facilities nearby. (Mongolia...*Hello?*)

So, the doctor said there was only one alternative: he would give me a crash course right there in the E.R. on how to remove the stitches myself. He took a needle and thread (they probably don't call it "thread") and began sewing stitches onto the white paper used to cover the examining table. He demonstrated how to grasp a stitch with tweezers in one hand, slide the open end of the scissors underneath with the other hand, and then clip the stitches individually, carefully extracting each one with the tweezers. Then, he instructed me to pour hydrogen peroxide on the wound frequently each day thereafter until the "bubbling" stopped, a sign that the wound was healing.

On the morning of my tenth day into the trip, I faced the reality that this was my day of reckoning. It was time to see what I was really made of (figuratively speaking). Fortunately, I was still in urban Mongolia and had not yet traveled to the Gobi Desert where we'd be stepping back in time to more primitive digs.

I went into the bathroom in my hotel room, flipped on the light switch and pulled my hair back, securing it with a hair clip. There was only an ice cold, factory-sealed bottle of water in the room for drinking. I knew that just wouldn't do. I hoped that the tap in the bathroom sink would provide water hot enough (and safe enough) so I could sterilize my version of surgical instruments—cuticle scissors and eyebrow tweezers.

I ran both of them under the steaming, hot tap water until my hair began to frizz from all the humidity. (That seemed sterile enough to me.) I turned off the faucet and then poured a generous splash of hydrogen peroxide over the "instruments". Then, I clipped and pulled out each stitch, one by one, exactly as I had been taught during my ten-minute medical school training. I finished the procedure by squeezing more hydrogen peroxide onto my forehead through a saturated cotton ball. It stung just a little bit, but not much to talk about (so I won't talk about it). Suffice it to say—I lived.

I was pretty proud of myself in the end. So, I guess the heading of this section should have been entitled, "How the Teacher Taught *Me*"!

– SEVEN –

How to Bathe While Bandaged or in a Plaster Cast

Something no one teaches you is how to successfully bathe when *both* feet are bandaged following surgery. I had undergone bunion removal, metatarsal repair and hammertoe surgery on both feet at the same time. (Don't ask.) I think I just was afraid I wouldn't go back later for surgery on the other foot if I had time to think about it while the first one was healing. I had several weeks of vacation and sick days piled up from my job, so it seemed like a good idea at the time.

The surgeon warned me that using plastic bags to protect the bandages while bathing doesn't work because the bags always leak. He cautioned that there's no efficient way to take other than a "sponge" bath for a while. That wasn't at all appealing to me, given the fact that I expected to be bandaged for two whole weeks until the stitches were removed.

So, genius that I am, I stepped into my empty bathtub wearing only my surgical shoes and a smile. I sat down carefully, positioned my left foot up on the tub rim and my right foot up on the other rim, and then filled the bathtub. Voila! (It probably resembled a low-budget, X-rated movie scene, but it worked, nevertheless.) When I finished bathing, I simply drained the water, put my feet back down on the empty tub floor, pulled myself up to a standing position and got out. Dry feet!

CB ❧ CB ⁊ ❧ ⁊

About a year later, my mother had taken a trip to Philadelphia to visit my sister and her family. Unfortunately, during her stay, she fell and broke her hip, necessitating a five-week recovery and rehabilitation stint before returning home to Chicago. I decided that her time away would be a prime opportunity for me to have one foot operated on again to correct a problem stemming from a previous surgery. I reasoned that I would have no one else to take care of at home and would be healed sufficiently in order to take care of my mom by the time she returned. Plus, bathing again while bandaged would be a snap, now that I had a system in place.

After the five weeks passed, I went to the airport to pick her up and arranged for a wheelchair to be delivered right to her seat on the plane. I waited at the far end of the jetway until everyone else had deplaned so they could bring her out. (Now, mind you, I hadn't said anything to her about my surgery during her absence because I wanted her to just focus on her own recovery.)

On board the plane, my mother was asked if

someone were picking her up, and she replied, "Yes, my daughter."

"Could she be on crutches?" the flight attendant asked.

Not missing a beat, my mother casually responded, "Knowing her, *anything's* possible."

Well, there she was in her wheelchair and I, on my crutches. The flight attendant looked us over and said, "I think I'd better order a wheelchair for you, as well."

That she did, but there were no chariot races this time as in Roanoke, just a nice, long opportunity to catch up on five weeks' separation as we rolled down the concourse side by side.

CR ❧ CR 80 ❦ 80

Now, back to bandaging. Bathing or showering with a bandaged wrist is not as simple an event as it had been with my foot surgeries. I underwent carpal tunnel surgery on each wrist, but only one at a time, thank you very much. (I'd learned my lesson!) If you really watch what you're doing, you *can* bathe and still keep the bandages dry.

All it takes is a surgical glove (preferably, size "Large", but "One-Size-Fits-All" works, too), masking tape and a little patience. You have to employ the "one use" rule, however. Those plastic gloves don't last for much longer than one use, and paper masking tape barely makes it through the one time. But, there's nothing like a real bath or shower to pick up your spirits for the day ahead.

Shampooing hair while bandaged is not as difficult as it might seem. The trickiest part for me was figuring out how to manage both the shampoo bottle and my bandaged hand at the same time. The problem was easily solved by first shopping at one of those warehouse superstores for a gargantuan-sized bottle of shampoo.

You'll need the whole bottle in the shower, so get used to the weight of it in your healthy hand. You have to hoist the bottle, upend it and hold it against the tiled shower wall with your good hand. Cup your gloved, bandaged hand beneath the bottle opening and put pressure on the bottle by pushing your head into it, squeezing out just the amount of shampoo you'll need. Now, put the bottle down and commence lathering. (It's easier than it sounds, believe me, and you can always take an aspirin later if it gives you a headache.)

CB&CRSO&SO

Lymphodema is a swelling of an extremity (usually the arm) following removal of lymph nodes in connection with cancer surgery or radiation treatments. There is a strict protocol followed at the beginning of treatment. Several layers of bandages are used to immobilize the arm so that it appears as if encased in a cylinder. (If you want to see a picture of this, check out vascularweb.org.) Combined with daily exercises and "soft tissue" massage of the arm and torso, the flow of lymph is directed away from the armpit, and bandaging between treatment sessions prevents further swelling by compressing the limb.

Confused yet? Well, that's all I intend to say about how it works, so don't worry about it. I just wanted to lay a little groundwork. The treatment ran for five consecutive days at a physical therapy facility. I'd spend two to three hours there daily, including the time it took for rebandaging (which I had to keep on overnight until I returned the next day for more treatment). The bandages wrapped around each finger individually, pretty much immobilizing them, and ended finally at the shoulder of the affected arm. They were several layers thick and, of course, I chose the hottest week of the year to begin my therapy.

So, my treatise on "how to bathe while bandaged" doesn't apply here at all. I couldn't even use a surgical glove to keep dry because even the largest size didn't fit over the bandages. (Visualize a mummy.) After carefully getting into the bathtub while balancing on the other hand in order to sit down, I'd have to remember to hold my bandaged arm up (as if stopping traffic) while I'd bathe the rest of me.

Here's where it got tricky—rinsing off. I remembered the traffic cop part, but as I gently leaned back in the tub to rinse off, I completely forgot that the *underside* of my upper arm was bandaged up to my shoulder. I also forgot that the combination of Ace bandage, plus soft, cotton bandage, plus gauze bandage would act like a blotter when wet and soak me to the skin! (I could actually watch the wetness travel up my arm from elbow to shoulder like a transparent lava flow from an active volcano as I yelled "Noooooo!!!")

I tried using my hair dryer, but that didn't work. I got dressed and tried to stand outdoors to dry, but I lasted only a minute in the 90° sweltering heat. That made me feel even more uncomfortable. So, I just went to physical therapy "as is" and explained when I arrived why the dressing was wet.

My physical therapist said she couldn't put the wet bandages in the towel dryer while I was receiving treatment because the heat would stretch out the rubberized bandages. She'd just have to charge me for new ones because she had to reapply them after my treatment.

That's when I had one of my brainstorms. I told her I had just had my car washed the day before, and it was parked directly in front of the facility. She called one of the physical therapy aides into the room and listened as I instructed the aide to drape each bandage over the hood of my car for the sun to dry. Two hours later, my therapy was completed for the day, and my bandages were bone dry and ready to put back on.

The next morning I was doubly careful when taking my bath. But, wouldn't you know it? I let my guard down for one brief second as I was rinsing off, and I was soaked again from elbow to shoulder. I returned to physical therapy, my head hanging down sheepishly as I entered the place. When asked what was wrong, I just replied, "I guess I must be the Britney Spears of Physical Therapy: 'Whoops! I did it again!'" My physical therapist smiled and shook her head, then called in another aide to help me with the dressing.

I explained to the aide how we had dried the bandages the day before and pointed to my car, again parked right in front of the place. She scooped up all of my bandages, went outside and began streaming them over the length of my car just as I had explained. This caught the attention of two patients sitting in the reception area. They joined her outside and asked if she were "T.P."ing my car. When she explained to them what she was really doing, they offered to help her. The three of them rolled out the bandages onto the hood, secured them under the windshield wipers and then trailed them up and over to the trunk of the car, laughing all the while. (That was my indirect contribution toward lightening the weight of everyone's day.)

- EIGHT -

Other Stuff You Can't Do (For a While)

There are many everyday tasks that you simply cannot perform just after having surgery. Most of them involve skills requiring physical dexterity or performing tasks such as bending/grasping/lifting/ putting on your eyebrows, and the like.

Here is a typical list of the things I personally could not accomplish right away, so if you're about to undergo surgery, prepare yourself for much of the same. I also offer some tips which I hope will be helpful on how to work around these temporary setbacks:

Using a toothbrush with your dominant hand if your arm is in a cast or bandaged

The obvious solution is to use your other hand, but be forewarned! Unless you have developed good manual dexterity ahead of time, be prepared to almost put your eye out the first time, as I nearly did. (Can mint toothpaste cause blindness?)

Putting on makeup with your dominant hand if your arm is in a cast or bandaged

Unless you're employed by Ringling Bros., Barnum and Bailey, you may not be at all pleased with your results from the beginning. Grasping is the skill you'll want to develop in order to avoid the "Bozo, the Clown" look as you apply your makeup.

Wearing pantyhose when one leg is in a cast

You have to employ a little creativity here and cut off one leg of the pantyhose just below the knee part. Carefully ease the cut stocking up and over the cast without snagging it (not always possible), and then tuck the raw edge of the stocking into the cast. Put the other leg of the pantyhose on as you would normally. (You'll have people wondering all day long how you got a pair of pantyhose on *under* the cast.)

And, if you hate wasting anything or are just plain cheap, you can use the remaining foot part of the stocking you just cut off to repel moths in your pantry or kitchen cabinet. Just fill it with peppercorns and tie a knot in the end. Hang up the pepper-filled "sachet" in the pantry or cupboard and it will repel moths naturally, without any poison. (Tip for the day—courtesy of Joey, the Green Grocer, from my neighborhood supermarket.)

Signing checks when your hand is in a cast or bandaged

Sign several checks before you have your surgery, but then remember to keep them in a safe place!

Vendors will accept checks signed with an "X" or signed by your other hand if you're able to do that. I found it easier to just sign a few of them ahead of time and then have the merchant fill in the rest of the check data. Remember to tell them to "press hard" if you have duplicate checks so you can update your check register later in private. (You don't want a stranger seeing that bizillion-dollar balance in your checkbook.)

Wearing one high-heeled shoe and one surgical shoe

If you're a fashion maven and have to look "smart" wherever you go, at least consider wearing a lower-heeled shoe on your healthy foot. Otherwise, you'll look dopey...*and* you'll limp due to the uneven height. The Fashion Police will give you a pass when they see you're wearing a surgical shoe. (If you're *really* nuts, do what I did and have both feet operated on at the same time. The result—two surgical shoes and double the amount of compassion you get normally.)

Zipping up pants when your dominant hand is in a cast or bandaged

The only practical solution is to wear pants with an elastic waistband until your recently operated-on hand regains strength and dexterity. Even if you return to work and require more business-like attire than sweat pants, you can wear a shirt or blouse *over* the pants rather than tucked in (another task not easily performed by the affected hand).

I've developed the "skill" of zipping up with the other hand, although I probably look more like a contortionist than someone just trying to get dressed. So, if you're not particularly adept at using your non-dominant hand, an elastic waistband is the way to go.

Climbing up stairs to the second floor when your leg is in a cast or bandaged

I had never lived in a house with a second floor before moving into the one I live in now. A house with bedrooms upstairs seemed like such a refreshing idea after a lifetime of first-floor living. But, if your leg is in a cast or is immobilized by bandages, climbing those stairs becomes a daunting task. Unless you want to do the "baby steps" routine (placing both feet on each stair so that by the time you do reach the second floor, you've forgotten why you went up in the first place), take up residence downstairs for as long as you can.

I didn't even attempt to climb my sixteen stairs to the second floor, but resigned myself instead to sleeping on the sofa bed in the family room for the two weeks. When I finally got the stitches removed, I asked the male nurse if I could bathe now, and he just replied, "Yes, please."

Cutting the grass with an electric lawnmower while you're on crutches

It's awkward enough to mow the lawn without cutting the cord attached to the electric lawnmower (as I did the first time I ever used one). Even if you're normally proficient at mowing the lawn, ask a kindly neighbor to do it for you until you're able to do it yourself once again. Remember, a lawnmower won't prevent you from weight bearing when crutches are intended for that purpose. It's more important to heal than have your lawn look tidy and ready for "Home and Garden". (Besides, you won't have to ask that nagging question always on a woman's mind: "When I push a lawnmower, do these crutches make me look fat?")

Opening new jars when your hand is in a cast or bandaged

Unless your non-dominant hand is particularly strong and can pick up the slack while you're healing, ask someone to open new jars (or peel potatoes or oranges or open new packages of cereal or crackers) for you. That's when developing a good relationship with one's neighbors comes in "handy". (Pun intended.) Don't forget to offer them a cracker.

Closing the driver's side car door when your left arm is in a cast or bandaged

At the risk of compounding a problem by falling out of the car while trying to wrestle the door shut, just tie a rope or a belt to the inside handle and pull on that with your right hand to close the door. You may have to get creative if you don't have a door handle that will accommodate a "pull cord", however. You might try getting into the car, rolling down the window with your right hand (I hope you've got power windows), calling out the window to anyone nearby, and asking them to please be a dear and close your door after you're in.

Putting on pantyhose if your arm or hand is in a cast, using a Q-tip with a casted arm, hooking your bra the "regular way" with a casted arm

Just forget it!

CR ❧ CR&ED ⸖ ED

As I implied earlier, this is not an all-inclusive list. There certainly are other challenges that may crop up which I haven't listed here. I just don't want to spoil the surprise for you.

– NINE –

"X" Marks the Spot

When you're admitted into a hospital for surgery, it seems you're asked a multitude of times which body part is going to be operated on. Don't let it bug you. It's for your own protection. Mistakes have been made at times due to lack of staff/patient communication (but at *other* hospitals, not at mine, of course).

There are horror stories about hospital personnel writing a big "X" on the patient's limb slated for amputation, only to discover afterwards that the surgeon mistakenly assumed "X" meant "NO" and amputated the *other* limb. One surgeon of mine would print his initials, KGD, with a felt marker on the leg to be operated on. (Narcissistic, I suppose, but effective, nevertheless, since it meant that this leg was his to work on. I even joked with him that it was a good thing his last name wasn't something like "Bennett" or "Brown". Otherwise, he could be accused of being a member of the Russian KG*B*.)

Writing the word "YES" (either by the patient or hospital staff member) is another accepted way to communicate which body part is to be operated on. And, even using this code word, you'll still be asked several times for verification before you're finally wheeled into the operating room.

The first time I saw the word "YES" was when I had breast cancer surgery. After confirming with me which breast was to be operated on, the nurse had me write "YES" with a felt marker on the affected one. I even wrote it upside down (from *my* vantage point) so it would be as plain as day to whomever read it. I had to wait a long time for the surgeon to arrive, however, and was beginning to lose my nerve. I peeked down my hospital gown, and the nurse asked what I was doing. I said I had been waiting so long that I was just checking to see if the word had changed from "YES" to "MAYBE".

෦෫෨෨෨෦ඁ෨

A surgeon whom I had seen just a few times always seemed to act quite detached toward me, almost unfriendly. When he spoke, it was in the briefest of sentences, as if just tolerating me (or perhaps he just was lacking in social skills). He was purported to be an excellent doctor but didn't seem to waste his time on small talk. So, when the word "YES" was written on my arm in pre-Op, I was sure it was an acronym for "**Y**oung **E**gotistical **S**urgeon". (He had many other good qualities, the O.R. nurse assured me, and I eventually found that out for myself. So, I take it back.)

I always had to wait a significant amount of time to

see him, though, before each office visit. The phone call came on the morning of surgery letting me know that he was "running early", and I was asked to come in as soon as possible. I was halfway torn between getting there as soon as I could or waiting until my originally scheduled time, just to show him it works both ways. But my growling stomach convinced me that the sooner my surgery was over, the sooner I could eat something. "Nothing by mouth after Midnight" isn't too bad when you have an early morning surgery, but mine had been scheduled for the afternoon.

I dressed hurriedly and got to the hospital, changing into the universal open-back hospital gown and slipper socks (cocoa color with white foot treads). I got up on the hospital gurney and made myself comfortable, expecting a short wait. I should have remembered that old saying, "Hurry up and wait", because things run smoothly only in a perfect world.

The minutes ticked by, and I waited and waited. I was given something to "relax me" and then passed the time by letting my eyes wander about the room. I checked out the hospital décor as I lay there and then eavesdropped on the nurses' conversations. I must have started to drift off to sleep but not before seeing one of the nurses point toward me and thinking I heard her say the word, "coroner". I sat bolt upright on the gurney and said, *"Coroner?"*

But, the nurse replied, "No, dear. Your doctor's name is '*Cormer*'. He should get here soon." He did— an hour later.

જી⭒ભ૪૭⭒ૐ

Anyone who's ever watched a medical drama on TV knows they play music in the operating room. I suspect it's the surgeon's taste that prevails as to what music is played, or at least it ought to be. After my own comfort, the person I want to feel most relaxed and at ease is the surgeon. (I remember asking once, as I lay there shivering, why they had to keep it so uncomfortably cold in the operating room. Besides the fact that germs probably couldn't survive in such an environment, the surgeon explained that the overhead lamps are very hot, and it wouldn't be too cool if he dripped sweat on me as he operated.)

I used to work with someone whose good friend was an anesthesiologist. He tells the story of a ninety-year-old man who "coded" on the operating room table during surgery (medical lingo for "his heart stopped"). They got out the defibrillator paddles and were able to resuscitate the old guy. Then, someone changed the music selection in the O.R. to that Seventies' Bee Gees' hit, *"Stayin' Alive"*.

Ever since hearing that story, I always request that song as I'm being wheeled into Surgery. Who knows if they really play it or not? But, no matter. It's still my lucky charm.

- TEN -

That Last Box of Christmas Ornaments

Never continue doing something when you begin to feel overtired. That's how I broke my ankle skiing. "Just one more run down the hill, okay?" *Not* okay! The same goes for taking down the Christmas decorations and putting them away for the season.

I had accomplished almost everything in one day, single-handedly taking down the outside holiday lights, the Christmas tree, garland, ornaments and tree lights, and all the other inside house decorations. I was getting tired but was on that last box. While up on the ladder, I tried to stretch, then hoist the heavy carton up and over the overhead garage door track to the top level of the shelves that line my garage wall.

Any rested person would have seen the folly in that

maneuver. But accidents happen in a split second, and rested or not, I wasn't able to regain my balance in time. I thought I was on the bottom rung of the ladder (how could I forget climbing up to the *third* rung?) and realized I couldn't steady myself in time, so I just stepped back, certain I was only inches from the floor. I landed hard, still cradling the box of ornaments in my arms as my right knee went sideways. I could feel it pop. I could *hear* it pop. That's not good. I set the carton down on the cement floor and tried to walk. Each time I tried to take a step, I fell down, eight steps in all before I stopped trying.

After spending the whole day working outside and then in the garage, I did what any self-respecting single woman too independent to call for help would do. I crawled up those sixteen stairs to the second floor, took a shower, re-did my hair and make-up (you never know when you're going to meet "Mr. Right" or even "Mr. Close Enough"). Then, I drove myself to the Emergency Room—yes, using my right leg.

It was a Sunday night, and no one there really seemed to know what was wrong with my leg. (I found out later that they don't diagnose in the E.R., they just "treat 'em and street 'em".) They placed me in an "immobilizer" cast that went from my ankle to my thigh, secured by Velcro straps. I could remove it at bedtime, and I was instructed to see my own doctor the next day. (What a complete and total waste of makeup!)

Oh, did I mention that when I finally got the bill from the hospital, a $24.00 charge appeared on it for being seen on a Sunday night? I called to enquire about the charge, certain there had been a mistake. But, I was told that the charge was legitimate and that they have a "surcharge" for holidays, as well. Now, this is a regular open-24-hours-a-day hospital, not a private urgent care facility. (Oh, yeah, I forgot. This is California where practically everything is "ala Carte".) The only upside to the day's events is that none of the ornaments in the carton got broken.

ℭℨ᷍ℭℜℨ᷍ℬ

It's a good thing I hung onto my crutches from my skiing accident years earlier, but I did need to replace the worn, rubber crutch tips. I left the hospital and drove to my local WalMart to buy replacements for the old, dried up tips on my vintage wooden crutches (I never throw anything away) which crumbled with every step I took. No luck. They had everything for sale from Q-Tips to Cheese Nips, but no crutch tips.

So, I got back in the car and drove a couple miles further to Walgreen's. Of course, late Sunday night is when they mop the floors, right? The clerk saw my condition, told me to wait where I stood, and offered to get the replacement tips for me. He even put them on the crutches for me before I left the store. (Now, we're cookin'!)

The next day I called the orthopedic surgeon whose name I was given in the Emergency Room. He couldn't see me until late in the day, and not at his office located just a mile from my home. So, I got back into the car and drove to his other office, thirteen miles away. He examined my knee and said it could be a lot of things, but sometimes Mother Nature heals without the need for any outside intervention. I told him I couldn't stand on it without falling (even offering to demonstrate) and that I really needed help right now, no offense to him or Mother Nature.

He ordered an MRI finally (at my suggestion), but

that didn't happen for three more days. I was put back into the immobilizer cast and was released to go back to work. Ultimately, the MRI results revealed that I had torn both my medial and lateral meniscus (knee cartilage) and would require surgery to repair it. (So *there*, Mother Nature!)

Now, technically, you're not supposed to drive a car if you can't bend your right leg. But, I had to wait almost four weeks until the surgery date, and there were people to see, places to go and bills to pay. So, I went back to work a couple days later in my immobilizer cast (a twenty-four mile drive on the freeway) and toughed it out for the next month.

– ELEVEN –

Dr. "Hottie": Everyone Deserves at Least One

I met my first "hot" doctor at the hospital in Roanoke, Virginia. He was young, blonde and movie-star handsome. (I'd add "tall" to the mix, but everyone appears tall when you're lying down, so I can't be sure.) Just looking at him, though, took my mind off my troubles. I had double vision from my head injury and subsequent brain surgery, but seeing *two* of him was certainly no cause for complaint. I don't know if it's the "uniform" or what, but there's nothing like a man in hospital scrubs to bring out the blue of his eyes.

Of course, there's more to assessing a doctor than how he looks in scrubs. There's his skill level, of course, and the all-important bedside manner, that combination of compassion, patience and innate personality to complement his actual technical skill. He might be the most highly trained physician, proficient at what he does, even famous. But the package seems incomplete unless his procedural skill is blended with empathy, sensitivity and that ability to lift the world off your shoulders, at least for a while. No, that's not being needy. I just believe that people respond better when a doctor's skills include patient nurturing.

CʒໞໞႸໞ

I remember one particular visit to the Emergency Room. I had been standing on a stepstool in my bedroom, adjusting the rod which held up my drapes. My mother was standing there beside me, gazing out the window. It was a hot summer day and, of course, everyone was wearing shorts to keep cool—I mean *everyone.*

We were having a conversation, when all of a sudden, she said, "Oh, my gosh! Look at those two fat asses walking down the street—and in *shorts,* no less."

I looked away from what I was doing for just a brief moment in order to see what she was looking at, and I lost my balance and tumbled off the stepstool. I hit my head (yes, again) on the windowsill and cut my ear open. It looked like I would require stitches, so we headed off to the hospital.

The name of the attending physician in the Emergency Room wasn't exactly a confidence builder—it was Dr. Savage. No lie. He lived up to his name, too, because, not only was he aloof and personality-free, but suturing must not have been his strongest suit in med school either. (I can still notice his handiwork today when I look in the mirror.)

CB &~ CREO ~ EU

I've found that orthopedic surgeons, in general, seem to keep a fair distance between themselves and their patients. I've heard it said that the more detached they remain, the more focused they're able to be. In my opinion, they could be even more effective if their demeanor weren't so impersonal and "all business" and if a measure of warmth and support were sprinkled in alongside their technical proficiency.

One orthopedic surgeon I had impatiently snapped at me when I hesitated in answering his question about my return to work date.

He brusquely asked, "Ms. Langer, can you *work* or can you *not?*"

I told him that I probably could return to work, but not without still being in some pain.

He curtly responded, "Well, then you *cannot!*" (End of discussion.)

Another surgeon made it "all about him". I don't think he was aware he did that, but it surely put me off at the beginning.

No matter what I told him about my knee injury, he'd say, "*I* had that."

Then he'd go into a recounting of how he injured his own knee during his college football-playing days. And, his patient care coordinator was just like him.

When I told her I had just been diagnosed with breast cancer, she said, "Oh, *I* had that." (Was this an omen of what was to come if I continued treatment with them? Did I have to be stricken with terminal "cooties" in order to direct the focus away from them?)

I had the surgery to repair my knee, and then it happened. Five months after tearing the meniscus, I slipped on a melted ice cube while in the lunchroom at work. I re-tore the same medial and lateral meniscus and required surgery once again to repair them.

I went back to the same surgeon, and he said, "Congratulations. You're now a member of the 'Five Per Cent Club'. Only five per cent of people who ever tear a meniscus ever tear it again. *I* also tore mine twice." (Here we go again!)

I was still trying to absorb the news he had just given me, and I asked, "How could it happen *again*?"

He said, "Well, the first time it happened, I was playing football in college. The second time, I was getting out of a car and missed the curb..."

I interrupted him and said, "No, not you. *Me!*"

છ⋙⊙⋘ જી

A surgeon I had seen over several months always addressed me formally as "Ms. Langer" instead of using my first name. I assumed the first time he did that was because he didn't want to presume it was all right to call me by my first name since we had just met.

I corrected him, though, and said "You can call me 'Annette'" (which he promptly ignored and then went on with the exam in silence).

On my first follow-up visit after the surgery, he walked into the room and greeted me, again using my last name.

I said, "It's really okay to call me by my first name."

He responded, "I call everyone by the last name so I don't have to remember who prefers last name or first name." (Now, how much effort would it take to write it at the top of the chart or use some other reminder?)

I was determined to make him bend a little and decided to use some humor to break the ice.

As he focused his attention on the long incision to check how it was healing, I asked, "Why does the scar look perfectly straight here and then veer left and then right again? Is that where you got the hiccups, or did you have to sneeze?"

As solemn and serious as can be, he merely gave a short answer about having to cut around, rather than through, a nerve. (C'mon, buddy! Unclench. I'm just kidding!)

છ ✦ ભ૪ભ ✦ ૪૭

There was one surgeon, though, whose personality was just the opposite. Not only was he a "hottie" by conventional definition, but he was also the poster boy for "great bedside manner". He always showed patience and good listening skills by rephrasing everything I told him so that I knew he really heard what I was saying.

Each visit began with a handshake, held long enough to make that connection. After the physical exam and a little more discussion, he'd end the visit by asking me if he had answered all my questions. Then he'd shake hands again in goodbye. I never felt that my examination was rushed because he always spent the time. If he were running late, he'd apologize upon entering the room and again at the end of the visit, saying, "Thanks for waiting for me." (Now, that's what I call good patient care.)

When a friend of mine visited from England, she came into the examining room with me.

At the end of the visit, Dr. "Hottie" turned to her and said, "Very nice to have met you, Debra", remembering her name.

When he first diagnosed my breast cancer, he put my finger on it so that I could feel the lump, but I still couldn't feel it.

I asked, "How is it that *you* can feel it, and I can't?"

He replied, "Well, I've been doing this for a lot of years."

"I know", I said, "but I've had these breasts longer than you've been in practice."

He just smiled and said, "Go and wait for me in my office. I'll just take care of the next patient, but I won't be more than five minutes, I promise. I want to spend some time with you." And he did—a full twenty minutes.

He sat down with me and offered to delay the discussion until I had a family member or significant other (I hate that term) present, if I preferred to wait. I suppose that's because when you're hit with the "C" word, your mind is reeling, and you might miss something. But I declined, and so he patiently explained what the mammograms and physical exam had revealed and then presented the array of treatment options open to me.

CB ❧ CBEO ☙ EO

The day I had the needle localization biopsy, as it's called, Dr. "Hottie" came into the operating room as the nurses were setting up a screen below my chin so I couldn't see what he would be doing. I was given a mild sedative to relax me before they administered the anesthesia. (Why the screen, then?) I protested a little when the divider was set up, saying, "Hey, that's like inviting me to Thanksgiving dinner and then making me sit in the kitchen while everyone else is in the dining room."

He said, "Hon, there's nothing about what I'm about to do to you that even remotely resembles Thanksgiving."

I wasn't the only one asking questions, though. On my pre-op order, it showed "breast biopsy", but my right leg clearly was encased in a removable cast. I assured the operating room nurses that my leg injury was just a "bonus" and would be taken care of at a later time. My current chart order was correct.

The biopsy results showed that the tumor was malignant. The decision came down to two choices: lumpectomy, defined by breastcancer.org as a procedure where just the tumor and the surrounding tissue would be removed, or mastectomy: take the entire breast. I asked if I had a choice, and Dr. "Hottie" said that I did. After explaining the pros and cons of each option to me, I selected the less invasive procedure, the lumpectomy. He would attempt just to excise the tumor and a small amount of surrounding tissue, but the breast would be spared. In a separate operation, he would remove four or five lymph nodes from my armpit for testing to see if the cancer were localized or if it had spread.

After telling him my choice, he said, "Good. You don't need a mastectomy."

I asked why he had given me a choice in the first place if he believed I didn't need the more extreme surgical procedure. He just said it had to be my decision, not his. I had to be comfortable with my choice.

I still had to sign an authorization form in the hospital, though, permitting him to do a mastectomy if it came down to that, after all. (In the words of that famous obsessive-compulsive, hypochondriac TV detective, Adrian Monk: "Oh, what a time to be me!")

CR&~CR&~&R

Only *I* would agree to three surgical procedures on the same day! Previously, Dr. "*I*-Had-That" had consulted with Dr. "Hottie" by telephone while I sat on his examining table, and they both agreed I'd be able to tolerate the multiple procedures. It was my idea, actually, and I suggested it to them for these reasons:

1. I would require only one period of hospitalization (the insurance company's gotta love that);
2. I would require only one anesthesia (see #1. above); and, most importantly,
3. I would be home from work recuperating from one surgery anyway, so why not two? (or three, as I found out later)

Everyone else thought I was crazy, but it turned out to be a good decision for all the reasons I'd given. The only hitch was that a total of eighteen lymph nodes had to be excised instead of the four or five Dr. "Hottie" originally suspected he'd remove. But, the pathology results indicated that all eighteen were negative which means that the cancer was localized and had not spread to the lymphatic system.

When I asked him how many lymph nodes I have, he just replied, "A *lot*."

So, bottom line: I don't even miss them.

I remember waking up in the hospital the next day, and my first awareness was a sensation of heaviness from the bandages constricting my chest. I peeked down my hospital gown to see if both "the girls" were still there, but could see only the bandages. Dr.

"Hottie" came in soon afterwards and assured me that everything went well and that he didn't have to perform a mastectomy. (Whew! Mental hug.)

Later, Dr. "*I*-Had-That" came in to see me. His first words to me as I lay there bandaged from knee to boob were, "Well, *you* look useless!" (What a charmer! See what I mean?)

CB ⋙ CRRD ⋘ ED

A few days after the surgeries, I developed huge bulge in my armpit the size of an egg. I called Dr. "Hottie's" office about it and was told to come in right away. I slipped into the stylish, paper half-gown I was offered and waited there in Examining Room #3 for my turn to be seen. (I *knew* I still had both breasts but as I sat there on the examining table, I wondered if I had developed "a third one".)

I envisioned that behind each examining room door awaited a patient whose condition corresponded to the number on the door: Door #2 would be Normal (two breasts) and Door #1 (well, you get the picture). And then there was me, "*Tri-Boob*", waiting behind Door #3.

It turned out to be, not a third boob, but a new malady that I christened "armpitus giganticus". Actually, it was called a "*seroma*" (a pocket of fluid that had accumulated in the armpit), a common occurrence following lymph node surgery but which had to be drained, nevertheless. Knowing it was still difficult for me to raise my arm, Dr. "Hottie" took it and rested it on his shoulder while he examined me. (I felt like telling him, "You know, with a little music, in some cultures this could be considered dancing." But, of course, I didn't.)

He drained the seroma with a huge syringe (large enough to knock out a Budweiser Clydesdale horse). He cautioned me to not get alarmed if it happened again, saying that some women get it three, even four times following lymph node surgery. (Oh, whoopee.)

Well, sure enough. The fluid returned a few days later, so I went back to his office to have the seroma drained once again. Dr. "Hottie" sent his patient care coordinator to another examining room to attend to someone and then turned his attention to my seroma. (Remember that old hit song of the late Seventies by the Knack called *"My Sharona"*? No? Well, Dr. Hottie didn't either—even after I sang a few bars. Too young. Too bad—great guitar riff.)

As he began to draw off the fluid, he said, "Uh-oh."

I said, "*That's* not something I want to hear from a surgeon. What's wrong?"

He answered, "I don't have anything to empty this into. Here, hold this."

With that, he went into the supply closet for a basin, and I just stood there holding the big horse needle in place *in* my armpit until he came back.

Then he said, "Okay, now switch with me", as he took the syringe back from me and handed me the basin to hold for him. (At the end of the visit, I asked for a discount on his bill since I had "assisted" him during the procedure.)

ଔନ୍ଦୁ ଔଯ୍ଞ ୴ନ

Sitting in Dr. "Hottie's" waiting room once, I passed the time by eavesdropping on two older ladies also waiting to see him. One was a long-time patient, I gathered, but the other was there for the first time. She was visibly nervous, and the first woman was trying to reassure her. The nervous patient asked what the other thought about him. The long-time patient had nothing but praise for him.

"I remember my first time here, years ago", she said. "I remember thinking he's *so* young. He walked into the examining room, and I thought: *'Doogie Howser'*. But, he's a *good* doctor. You'll like him." (Inwardly, I smiled in agreement.)

After almost a year of follow-up visits, I was sitting at home one day and decided to create a thank-you card on the computer for Dr. "Hottie". I gave it to him after my examination and also mentioned that, after checking my record of insurance payments made to him for the year, I found I still owed him ten dollars.

He just replied, "That's okay. Just give me a card and a hug now and then. That's all I need." (More than a year later, I spotted my card still tucked inside my medical chart.)

ᜅᜇᜒᜅᜐᜓᜐ

After first moving to California from Chicago, I was unable to obtain a primary care physician for a while. I did find a wonderful OB/GYN who was both skilled and caring. She happens to be the only female doctor I've ever had, other than the one who delivered me. But, since her practice is limited to "lady stuff", as comedian Ray Romano calls it, I wanted to secure an overall primary care physician, too.

I tried right from the beginning to get an appointment with a particular doctor who came highly recommended, again because of a good bedside manner in addition to being a skilled physician. He had such a busy schedule, though, that he often closed his practice to new patients (much like a mutual fund closes its doors to new investors when they have too much money on hand to invest wisely). You had to time it just right to find that window of opportunity when he was accepting new patients again.

On my third attempt in six years, I finally snagged an appointment with him. He had a good sense of humor, too, I soon discovered. That's something I always find appealing in a person, so I knew we'd get along great.

When I told him I'd been trying to see him for six years, he turned to his nurse and said, "Wow, are we *that* backed up?"

That broke the ice, and I knew then that the six years I'd waited for him to become my primary care physician had been worth the wait. He spent about forty-five minutes then taking my complete history.

After I had finished bringing him up to speed on all my medical issues, he said, "This is too hard. It was nice meeting you, but we're closing our practice tomorrow. Go away." He was just kidding, of course, and gave me a thorough examination, even my *back*.

"Hmm", he remarked. "You must not have spent any time out in the sun when you were growing up in Chicago—no moles." After he finished looking me over from head to foot, he said, "Gee, those are cute socks!"

He's been my doctor for a while now. If I develop a medical problem which has no clear-cut solution, he assures me that he will not give up until he finds out exactly what's wrong, and even more importantly, how to correct it. That, on its own, buoys my confidence in him.

Recently, after ordering tests that revealed my cholesterol was too high, he said, "I could give you a three-year prescription, but then you'd get lazy and never call in for an appointment, and I'd get lazy and never follow up with you to see how you're doing. By giving you just a six-month prescription, it keeps us both vigilant."

CB ᔥ CRஇ ᔦ ℬ

So, what makes a doctor a "hottie"? Sure, it most certainly can be his looks—the salt and pepper hair (salt's winning, by the way), the twinkling blue eyes, the lips which break into an easy smile. Or, it may not be his appearance at all, but just his personality, the ability to make that connection with you, to engender and sustain the trust you've placed in him.

Erma Bombeck once counseled, "Never go to a doctor whose office plants have died." Everyone deserves a caring doctor. Sometimes you just have to keep on searching until you find one of your own. And (paraphrasing actor, Kelsey Grammer) when you do, it's as precious as finding a Snickers Bar at a fat camp!

– TWELVE –

Radiation and the Cat

The next step following cancer surgery is meeting your Oncology team, the doctors who administer the next course of treatment. They determined that I would not require chemotherapy (thank you, God!) but *would* need thirty-four days of radiation to kill off any microscopic cancer critters undetected during the surgery. The treatment would take place five days a week over a period of seven weeks.

I was assigned to two doctors. My radiation oncologist supervised my actual treatments, and my medical oncologist would see me for follow-up office visits and blood tests at regular intervals over the next five years. (That's when you get the "all clear", if that's how it turns out.)

The radiation plan was pretty interesting. A week before the actual treatments began, I went to the facility to get my "mapping" done, a series of teeny, tiny pinpoints of tattoo on my breast to mark the perimeter of the radiation field. I had no idea what my tattoos would look like or if I would even be given choices. I envisioned a very quiet, sterile tattoo parlor with a wall of samples—traditional pictures of butterflies, flowers and hearts, or daggers, skulls and crossbones to appeal to the more macho patients. (Bikers get cancer, too, you know.)

The technician broke the news, however, that I would be given only a scattering of single dots. To this day, the marks just look like a blue ballpoint pen had skipped across my skin here and there, not even enough to play a decent game of "connect the dots". He also told me about a woman who actually had a butterfly tattooed on her stomach. She became pregnant, and one wing grew significantly larger than the other wing as her tummy expanded. From that time on, they only did the dot pattern, rather than a recognizable shape. (I'll bet he was lying.)

CBⲀⲀCⲀꙄⲀⲀꙄⲀ

A week later I returned to the facility and began the actual radiation. Lying on an examining table in what the oncologist called "the bathing beauty position", I was instructed to place my right hand behind my head and the other one touching my hip (*very* "Esther Williams-esque"). I had to lie very still with my head turned toward the opposite shoulder and then focus on a small ceramic cat that sat on a bookshelf across the room. (Oh, I get it—a *cat* scan!)

The treatment lasted just under a minute. Then, the

technicians repositioned the huge overhead radiation "zapper", and I'd receive another invisible burst, again less than a minute in duration. I went for twenty-eight days of these double doses (except for the weekends) at one hospital in town. I took the last six days of treatment at another hospital fourteen miles away. They had a super-duper, humongous machine at that facility that zapped me only once each day, again for just about a minute.

So, sixty-two doses later, my energy was literally sapped from all the zaps, but my course of radiation had finally come to an end. (Yea.) Having to do all that extra driving before work didn't help my energy level. I scheduled my appointments for early in the morning to minimize the amount of time I'd have to take off work, good and faithful employee that I was (but more about that later). My customary, twenty-four mile, freeway commute became thirty-eight miles for those final six days of treatment.

Besides walking around like a sleep-deprived zombie (do they *need* sleep?), the only other outward evidence of the radiation was the appearance of a deep-red sunburn over one breast. I was given special ointment to use after each treatment, just as you would after getting a bad sunburn. I was told the color would fade back to normal in time. (It's still fading, even as I peek.)

☙❧☙❧❧

When my radiation treatments were completed, the technicians presented me with a beautiful bouquet of "Congratulations, you made it!" flowers. A year later, I was heading for a routine visit in another department of the hospital when I came upon a man slowly plodding down the sidewalk, carrying his bouquet. Our eyes met, and I said, "Congratulations. I got my bouquet last year." He just forced a little smile and nodded, too weakened to even speak.

Radiation may kill off any unseen cancer gremlins, but it surely depletes all of your energy in the process. I was assured, though, that in time, my energy level would return to normal. It has.

- THIRTEEN -

Taking Your Medicine...And Other Advice

Following your doctor's instructions to the letter (or almost) is a challenging test of wills. The task becomes even more daunting when you have multiple health care providers. You have to remember to tell each of them what the others have prescribed, whether that's medication or activity.

A surgeon I had would dole out painkiller after painkiller to me like he was operating a narcotics candy store. I know he didn't want to see me in pain, but I wanted him to fix what was wrong, not mask it with drugs. I've never been one to take a lot of medication, so I "went off my meds" frequently, as they say in the health care world. I just felt foggy all the time (or at least more so than usual). Eventually, I left that doctor's care because I lacked a basic confidence in him. (And, I didn't want my next vacation to be to the Betty Ford Clinic.)

One drug I was sorry to see go, however, was the hormone replacement therapy I had been taking for menopause. But surviving a bout with cancer put an end to that, and I was no longer permitted to take the drug. I missed it, too, because it really combated the hot flashes I have which sometimes run rampant. They come without warning, and I never know when I'm about to experience the next "power surge". But from that time on, I just became determined to think of those hot flashes as "my inner child playing with matches", as someone once said, and learn to deal with it.

CB❦C88O❧8O

When I first became troubled with carpal tunnel syndrome, I created what I termed a "pain chart" to present to the doctor to better explain the symptoms I was having. It was a very scientific chart, I might add, and I was very proud of it.   (Well, actually, it was just two sheets of 8½" X 11" graph paper joined together with cellophane tape.)

Unable to sleep one night because the pain was almost unbearable, I got up and decided to record my pain levels on paper. I detailed precisely the degree of pain I was having at its mildest, mid-range and worst intensity, the specific location of the pain and the direction it traveled. I placed my arm flat against the graph paper on the desk and traced an outline of my arm on it with a pen. Then, I took three, broad, felt-tip markers and started coloring in the areas on the chart where I was having the pain— yellow for "mild" pain, orange for "moderate" and red for "Help! I can't take any more of this!"

When I gave the drawing to Dr. "Hottie" at my next

appointment, he studied it for a while and then said "This is actually pretty cool!"

He was able to tell immediately what was causing the pain, just based on the placement of my colorful markings on the chart. Then, he referred me to a neurologist for a nerve conduction velocity test to clinically confirm what he suspected was causing my pain—carpal tunnel syndrome.

The diagnosis was corroborated by the neurologist, and both doctors agreed that surgery would be the best way to alleviate my painful symptoms. I asked Dr. "Hottie" if he would perform the surgery, but he said he wanted to refer me to a surgeon who did nothing but hands and wrists all day long. So, I asked if I could have my pain chart back to give to the new guy.

He smiled and said, "No. This is mine. Let him get his own chart." (Eventually, I did make another one for the hand surgeon.)

ෆ෮ඏ෧ඐ෨෮

After having knee surgery to repair the torn meniscus, the doctor prescribed several visits for physical therapy. My treatment consisted of soft tissue massage, ultrasound and exercise, using the various pieces of gym equipment at the facility under the direction of the physical therapist. That was followed by electrical stimulation of the muscle groups while my knee was wrapped in an ice blanket (which, by the way, I hated). I was directed to do about fifteen exercises at home, as well—ten repetitions each, three or four times a day. (Yeah, right.)

At my next appointment with the knee surgeon, he said, "Look. Let's get real. I'll be happy if you do them at home even *three* times a week."

I tried to be as compliant as I could, but I'm a whiner at heart, and in the beginning it was pretty hard to remain faithful to the program.

CB☙CRSD☙EU

Speaking of programs, regaining hand and wrist strength following carpal tunnel surgery is a laborious task that requires developing manual dexterity, concentration, endurance and a huge dose of patience. At first, your hand is too weak to grasp even a one-pound weight to do the strength training exercises, let alone lift anything heavier.

My physical therapist started me off grasping a six-ounce tomato paste can to increase wrist motion, extending it forward to mimic knocking on a door, then sideways, then other positions, as tolerated. This was part of my routine at the physical therapy facility, but I was encouraged to continue these and other muscle strengthening assignments at home, too, between visits. I slowly, but surely, graduated to an eight-ounce tomato sauce can, but neither of these physical therapy "tools" lasted very long in my arsenal of home gym equipment.

Some people find it soothing to play music or watch TV while doing strength training. Me? I tended to find either of those distracting and preferred peace and quiet in order to concentrate on the task at hand. So, I'd just sit there in silence at the kitchen table and let my mind rest while performing my exercises. But, my thoughts tended to wander after a while, rather than staying focused on counting the number of "reps", as I was taught. A little onion and garlic, a little oregano and thyme, and before I knew it, I had repurposed the "weights" and was busily making pasta sauce on the stove.

– FOURTEEN –

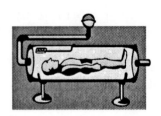 

Tests I Hate

I don't care how handsome or wonderful or charming your doctor is. I don't care if they serve caviar and champagne while you're waiting your turn to be treated. There are still some hospital tests that no one looks forward to, no matter what the prize.

After age fifty, you're supposed to have a colonoscopy at least once in your life. (Like, who'd voluntarily want *more* than one?) Well, I put off having mine for years but finally did make the appointment to have it done. I was told I'd have to "prepare" for it—no solid foods for twenty-four hours before the procedure, only clear liquids (like yellow gelatin and broth), and, of course, the dreaded "nothing at all by mouth after Midnight".

I also had to take an oral enema, a liquid solution to drink at Noon and then again at 6:00pm. (I don't want to get too graphic here in case you're snacking as you're reading this, so let's just be polite and call it "liquid dynamite".) I had a class that evening that I really didn't want to miss, so I amended my program, taking the first dose at 3:00pm and the second at 9:30pm when I got home. I got through the class without incident, but I was up *all* night "cleansing" my system so I'd be squeaky-clean empty for the colonoscopy the next day.

I dragged into the hospital the next morning and got prepared for the procedure in the pre-Op room. I was assured by the staff that I "wouldn't feel a thing". I assured them in return that my butt was so numb from the "activities" of the day before that I couldn't help but feel nothing.

I was given an anesthetic anyway, so the next memory I have of the event is the doctor saying to me afterwards, "Well, I found a little something, but I don't believe you need surgery for it. Just up your fiber, and that should take care of things." (I felt like saying, "Up *yours!*")

Recently, I had occasion to see one of the other doctors in his medical practice. The "butt doctor" walked out of his office and nodded hello as he passed me on my way to the examining room, but his expression told me didn't recognize me. (I wasn't surprised. He probably never looked at my face the first time we met.)

CB ∾ CRED ∾ RD

When I was initially diagnosed with breast cancer, it was just after having a routine mammogram that women are supposed to get every year once turning forty in order to prevent cancer, or at least detect it early. I remember the first time I ever heard the word "mammogram". I thought, "Hmm...It's probably like a 'candygram' for boobs." (Who knew it would turn out to be the anti-Christ of fun times?)

If you never have had the delightful experience of having a mammogram, let me describe it to you. Imagine that your finger is in a vise and someone is turning the handle on the vise to try to flatten your finger. Or, how's this? Imagine that you're barefoot, and a car has just run over your foot. Then, the car backs up and runs over your other foot. Now, go somewhere in between, and that's what a mammogram feels like (to me).

So, I had my annual mammogram and several days later received a postcard in the mail instructing me to return for another one. (Oh, goodie. Two in two weeks.) I just assumed I must have moved and that they had to repeat the test to get a better reading. When I returned, the technician just said they wanted to take a different view. I tolerated the mammogram once again, secure in the knowledge that I wouldn't have to go through it again until a year later. (Wrong!)

This time the results clearly showed an abnormality, and I was urged to call my doctor right away. My OB/GYN referred me to a surgeon (Dr. "Hottie"), and shortly after that, I went into the hospital to have the surgical biopsy under sedation. That type of biopsy would provide more definitive information in my case than what a "needle biopsy" would reveal (which is normally performed in the doctor's office).

I can't totally explain the mechanics of the procedure, but this is what I remember. The radiologist injected dye into my breast through a syringe, and then he took the mammogram. He waited awhile, more dye, another mammogram, waited, blah, blah, blah—for a total of *seven* mammograms! By that time, my breast felt so flattened that, if it were detachable, we could have played a game of Frisbee with it in the parking lot. Then, I still had the surgical procedure to look forward to. God bless anesthesia because I'd had it for the day. (Just do what you have to, and wake me up later!)

Once, while I was midway through having my annual mammogram, the technician proceeded to tell me about a patient she had the week before. Apparently, the woman was so nervous about having her mammogram that she actually fainted during the procedure. The technician saw the patient slump and tried to reach for her while simultaneously stretching out her leg to hit the release mechanism to free the lady's trapped boob and then catch her before she hit the floor.

By the time the tech finished telling me the story, I was feeling a little queasy myself, relieved that my own time in the meat press had come to an end.

CB ❧ CB ❧ ❧ CB

Here's another test I'm not all that crazy about. It doesn't hurt at all, but it bugs me, nevertheless. An MRI has the ability to see your body part in layers, like Superman's x-ray vision, only more detailed. I've had two kinds of MRI's. An "open MRI" means you're *not* enclosed in the machine that takes the readings, just as the name implies. But, in a "closed MRI", you lie on a mechanical table that slides you entirely into a huge metal cylinder for the readings, the inside of which is only a few inches from your face—a real challenge if you happen to be claustrophobic.

Personally, I didn't care one way or another, but the annoying part is the noise the machine makes when it's capturing the images. It's a nearly deafening "Woody Woodpecker" sound (well, I suppose I'm exaggerating, but the decibel level certainly is louder than you're used to). Some imaging goes on for seven or eight minutes at a time, and one has to lie perfectly still and not even swallow. (Try not swallowing when you're told not to. That's *all* you want to do.)

You're given a breather for only as long as it takes the technician to set up for the next image and to ask, "How ya doin' in there?"

But, you still have to stay in the tunnel until all the imaging is complete. I've been in the closed MRI tunnel for almost an hour. It might as well have been a lifetime. Boring. There is a series of clicks and rattles and knocking sounds, and you can hear it even though they give you headphones to wear. You can bring your own music or listen to CD's they provide to drown out the noise somewhat. But, my MRI's have always been scheduled early in the day. At that hour, I just want to go back to sleep, not listen to music. So, I guess I pay the price and have to tolerate the "woodpecker" noise. I suppose it could always be worse. Just imagine if it were a rooster!

಄ఞ಄ಞఞ಄ಞಞ

There are a couple of diagnostic tests I've had a few times during my carpal tunnel syndrome "era" that were really uncomfortable. I knew the studies were necessary, but I'd still rate them in the "Top Five" of unpleasant things I've ever had done to me.

The NCV (nerve conduction velocity) study measures how well a nerve conducts impulses by evaluating how fast the impulse travels along the nerve. (Already, it sounds hateful.) The doctor holds a probe against the skin which emits an electrical impulse to stimulate the nerve. (Think "electronic cattle prod" or being struck by lightning—repeatedly.)

Don't let them fool you. Using the words, *"impulse"*, *"stimulate"* and *"nerve"*, in the same sentence should be an automatic warning to you that it's just a fast-talking way to disguise *my* word, "pain". Each time the probe zaps you, it takes a reading. It doesn't matter how much you scream (just kidding...I only yelled) because only the machine's reading counts, not your drama.

An EMG (electromyography) is somewhat different because it tests the muscle instead of the nerve, and it's usually performed in conjunction with the NCV study. A small, thin needle is inserted into several muscles, and the doctor examines the muscles by checking the electrical signals that travel from the needle to the EMG machine. (Your arm is supposed to jump, like a puppet's strings being pulled.) Yep, it hurts, but only *if* you have tissue that still responds to pain. So, the "good news-bad news" with both the NCV and EMG studies is that you won't feel much pain at all if your nerves are already damaged. (Comforting, no?)

If my watered-down description doesn't do it for you, you can check out the University of Chicago website, http://millercenter.uchicago.edu/learnaboutpn/ evaluation/electodiagnostic/ncv.shtml. Feel free to wade through all the medical jargon there for a full explanation of these tests if it interests you. Otherwise, don't sweat it. (This won't be on the test.)

My meeting with the pain management specialist after the second time I endured the NCV/EMG studies was almost as bad as the tests themselves.

He suggested that, ultimately, I should undergo an anesthetic nerve block procedure to relieve my chronic pain before considering having carpal tunnel surgery again. He said he had heard of people having nerve blocks multiple times—as many as fourteen, in fact. Then surgery *still* might be inevitable. (And I'd want to do this, why?)

The doctor blah-blah-blahed on endlessly, and it seemed as though he were giving me the complete, unabridged history of nerve conduction. The more technical he became (as if lecturing to third-year med students), the more I found myself tuning out. I know he lost me by the time he hit mid-presentation. In the end, I decided against having the nerve block anyway.

CB ❧ CB℞ ❧ ℞

While not in fact a "test", what I really dislike is having the anesthesia needles inserted into my veins. I have very small "chicken" veins, they say, and it's not always easy to find a viable one into which a needle can be inserted. (Don't get queasy. That's as graphic as I'm going to get.)

When I had surgery on my left carpal tunnel, the nurse tried unsuccessfully to find a good vein. I told her my right arm was off limits to her because of the risk of Lymphodema after lymph node removal from that armpit.

She said, "I can't use your left arm because that's the one going to be operated on."

So, she tried, again without success, to find a vein—first in my left foot and then in my right. Finally, ~~Dracula~~ (oops, I mean, the anesthesiologist) came into the room to see what was taking so long. Without a word, he deftly inserted the needle into my jugular vein. As I drifted off, my last conscious thought was something about a full moon.

⚘⚘⚘⚘⚘

Is there anyone who actually looks forward to an eye exam? The part I hate most is that little puff of air they blast into your eye to check for glaucoma. But on an even more basic level, I find the whole idea of reading an eye chart while looking through various lenses annoying.

"Is this better or worse? How about *this*? How about the *last* one?" (Grrrrr! I don't *know!*)

After several selections, they all begin to look the same to me. Sometimes, I just feel like lying for fear of disappointing the eye doctor. Then there's the breath issue. Someone should tell these people about breath mints or mouthwash if they're going to work that closely to people's noses.

⚘⚘⚘⚘⚘

Have you ever wondered if a dentist truly understands your reply to a question when he has a million fingers and instruments in your mouth? Your "uh-huh" or "uh-uh" answers are obvious, of course, but I'm talking about questions that require a bona-fide, simple sentence response. If *you* can't understand your own reply, how can the dentist comprehend what you said?

I had a dentist once whom *I* couldn't understand. I assumed it was because he had been in practice for so many years. He seemed to have adopted the "language" of his patients, mimicking the guttural grunts and garbled responses that he heard throughout his many years behind the drill. I always had to mentally sit on the edge of my seat in order to decipher even the simplest comments he made while I was trapped in his dental chair.

The only activity more irritating to me than cracking the code of unintelligible dentist-speak is having dental x-rays taken. You'd assume, with all the advances in dental equipment over time, that someone could invent a comfortable x-ray holder. Whether the dentist uses the old-fashioned, cardboard type (and bending the corners does *not* help) or the new, only slightly improved, rubberized, softer (?) version, having an x-ray taken is not on my list of favorite pastimes.

Attempting to balance the x-ray holder in your mouth while holding your breath during the imaging and remaining perfectly still without gagging your head off is probably why many people fail to enjoy the whole dental experience. (Anyone ever think of inventing chocolate-flavored x-ray frames? That would distract *me* sufficiently to get through the episode.)

લ૭ த૭<ભજ<ゑ૭<ゑ

This chapter can't possibly end without talking about the Pap test, or Pap smear, as it's generally called. (Somehow, I always think of peanut butter and jelly or a bagel with cream cheese whenever I hear the word "smear".)

First, you're placed on the examining table (sans underwear) in the most unflattering, undignified position, one foot in each stirrup. (Remember that old song by America called "A *Horse with No Name*"? Well, if they wrote a song about *this* contraption, it could be entitled "A Stirrup with No Horse *or* Saddle".)

The "speculum" is the torture implement of choice in this procedure. Dorland's Pocket Medical Dictionary defines it as "an instrument for opening or distending a body orifice or cavity to permit visual inspection". I feel like I should be at an auto mechanic's shop with someone shouting, "Crank 'er open, Magee. I think she's low on oil." (Talk about checking under the hood!)

Finally, there's a very good reason why men should never take telephone messages at home. There's the tale of a woman who, returning from the doctor's office, found this note from her husband.

It read, "Someone from the Gyna Colleges called and said your Pabst Beer was fine. I thought you didn't *like* beer."

- FIFTEEN -

The "BMW's" and Other Wonderful Friends

The recounting of my medical adventures would be incomplete without devoting a chapter to those who helped me get through the months following my "surgical trifecta" (the breast cancer, knee and wrist operations).

When you're about to be discharged from a hospital, someone from the Social Services department comes to your room to make sure you have adequate assistance at home, should you need it.

You're asked such questions as, "Do you have a ride home?" (Yes.) "Do you have someone to stay overnight with you tonight?" (No.)   "Do you have someone to help you bathe?" (No.)   "Do you have someone to help you with your meal preparation/laundry/grocery shopping/blah, blah, blah?" (No, No, No and No.)

Finally, I'd gently say, "Look, I have a friend who is

a nurse practitioner, one who is a retired nurse, one is a psychologist, another, a dentist, and, yet another, a veterinarian. They're all just a phone call away, so I think I've got it covered if I need anything. But, thanks for asking."

CB ☙ CSℰ ❧ ℬᴑ

When I came home from the hospital after the breast cancer/knee surgeries, I took up residence in my family room on the first floor at the beginning, both during the day and at night. But, it still took some effort to get up and "crutch" through the house to answer the door. It seemed that, if the phone weren't ringing, the doorbell was.

Don't get me wrong—it was wonderful receiving all those floral deliveries, but eventually I realized I had to conceive of a way to minimize my trips to the front door. So, when friends called to say they were going to drop by for a visit, I'd have them call me from their cell phone when they were in my driveway. Then, I'd simply use my remote garage door opener at my bedside table, and they'd let themselves in through the unlocked back door. It sure saved a lot of wear and tear on my energy (although, eventually, I did have to replace the battery for the remote).

One time, after I started to feel better, I knew my cousin's wife was coming over for a visit, but it was still somewhat difficult for me to get up and walk to the door. So, I taped a little note on the front door that simply read:

>*Carol, the door is unlocked.*
>*Just come in.*
>*Rapists, burglars and other lowlifes—*
>*please ignore this message.*

CR♣CR⊗♣℧

My next-door neighbors are a special gift. I don't know what I would do without them. They brought me meals while I was home recovering from surgery, did my grocery shopping, took me for medical appointments and cut my lawn. They even cleaned up the blood stains on my bedroom carpet from a fall I took during the night three weeks after surgery on my right knee (just after having my carpets cleaned, of course). I had tripped over an exercise machine in the dark during the middle of the night and tore my *other* knee open (requiring stitches), trying to shield my just operated-on right knee from further injury. (Can you say "night light"?)

Whenever my neighbors travel, I take in their mail and newspapers until their return, usually enough to fill a large trash bag. They give me a printed calendar page showing where they'll be and for how long. At the bottom, there's always the personal message: *Leave by your door. No lifting!*

CR♣CR⊗♣℧

It's difficult, though, to be sick or injured if you're an independent cuss like I am. It's just hard for me to ask people for help most of the time. So, I try to spread my inconveniences around. Things get done, everyone feels involved, and I get more practice at not feeling guilty about asking for favors. (I know. It's just me. I can't help it.)

Family or other friends took me to church, shampooed my hair and cooked meals for me. They showered me with flowers, helium-filled balloons, little stuffed animals, boxes and boxes of candy (and even a hot fudge sundae!) while I continued to heal. During one follow-up visit with Dr. "Hottie", I told him that I suspected I was gaining weight. My bath towel seemed to be getting smaller and it was taking me longer to dry off in the morning.

He just nodded and said, "Inactivity...and too many get-well chocolates." (Well, maybe I didn't put on *that* much weight, but let's just be diplomatic and say that my clothing size has graduated from "Junior Petite" to "Junior Plenty".)

One year, I received a "fortysomething" tee-shirt gift for a birthday I celebrated in the hospital. It was a parody of that old TV evening soap opera called *"thirtysomething"*, but it also served as a gentle acknowledgement of my reaching a landmark decade. Still, I was a good sport about it and wore it now and then. But, when I reached my half-century birthday, I found a way to keep on wearing the shirt (only on birthdays, of course) and still be truthful. I took it to a local tee-shirt shop and had lettered on the back of it: *This is an old shirt.*

CVS &⋅CVSひ⋅⋅ひ

One of the perks of being injured is qualifying for a temporary handicapped-parking placard for the car. The problem is that it's good for only a maximum of three months, and the State of California DMV grabs six dollars for the privilege. (You can get it renewed for another three months with a doctor's certification, but you have to pony up another six bucks.) By the time you're really getting used to having preferred parking, the imaginary meter hits "zero", and your time is up.

But, during those three months, no matter where I'd

go with friends, someone would always say something like, "Oh, don't forget your handicapped card!" (Not "Don't forget your sweater, or your glasses, or your medicine", but Don't-forget-the-hall-pass-that-let's-me-park-right-up-front-because-I'm-hauling-you-around.)

And while we're on the subject of handicapped-parking cards, recently two permanent handicapped license plates caught my eye. One was on a car which also had a *ski* rack mounted to the roof, and the other one was a personalized handicapped license plate which just read, "Mental".

⊗⃟☙⸎⊂⊋⁊⃟⸎⊘

Now, the "BMW" title needs a little explanation. There are two amateur production theatres in town. One is a small eighty-four seat theatre, and the other is a much larger venue where all of the main stage plays and musical productions are presented. A few years ago, I had joined a sixty-voice singing group called "Broadway Chorus", an offshoot of the community theatre.

As part of our spring concert one year at the larger theatre, ten of us were performing a selection from "The Best Little Whorehouse in Texas". We played the parts of the "ladies of the evening" (complete with feather boas and garters) who were being evicted from their establishment by the sheriff as we crooned our plaintive song. Our names were going to appear in the program, and someone suggested we needed a group name.

I said, "How about the BMW's? What better name could there be for the "Broadway Mainstage Whores"?

So, the name stuck. To this day, if we're planning a group get-together such as an extra rehearsal or even just an outing for dinner or a movie, we'll email each other with the details for the next "BMW field trip".

About four months after the cancer/knee surgeries, a few of us participated in a charity walk benefiting the American Cancer Society. It turned out to be a four-mile walk which, under healthier circumstances, would be no big deal for me. But, I was determined to walk as much of it as I could, even though I wore a bulky knee brace and still walked with a cane. Several times during the charity walk, a local police car would drive by and slow down to ask if I wanted to get into the back seat. (Really, it was because I looked tired, not because they were trying to take me in. *Really*.)

When people sign up for charity walkathons or relays, you're always asked for a team name, so we gave the staff our "BMW" name, of course. Imagine our embarrassment, though, when we saw a huge, printed sign at the event thanking the corporate sponsors: Home Depot, Coldwell Banker and BMW. (I hope they got a tax write-off, at least!)

C3&CR80&80

I look back over the years with affection for all my various caregivers and well wishers. Each time I gaze at the row of little, stuffed animals now taking up residence on the entire length of the sofa bed in my guest bedroom, I think about the givers, and not the surgeries, that precipitated those gifts. Each one has its own story to tell, each one is a reminder of all the help and love I felt from the givers. And all those plush, stuffed toys are much easier on the eyes than the plethora of "souvenir" Ace bandages, crutches, walker, braces and splints tucked away somewhere in the back of the closet.

– SIXTEEN –

My Positive Past (So Far)

The easiest thing in the world to do is to put yourself down or lose your self-confidence in the face of adversity or setbacks—*if* you allow it. The act of not believing in yourself, or feeling undeserving of good things, is a strong and powerful way of keeping yourself in the same place, unable to move forward or find your way out of a particular struggle. Sometimes, you feel that you have absolutely no power over a situation, that you're at the mercy of external forces. You got exactly what you deserved, and you're not surprised by it.

In her book, "Trusting Yourself", author M. J. Ryan says that "people who believe the universe is friendly tend to be optimistic and joyful. They also tend to trust themselves. Things that go wrong are seen as temporary setbacks beyond their control, not proof that they are idiots or the world rotten. Consequently, they enjoy their lives." The author goes on to ask, "If you have an inner critic, why can't you have an inner booster?"

CB&~CR&O~&E0

Being a visual person, I needed to put that concept into practice in order to make it real for me. I'm not much for making lists of "Pros" and "Cons", hoping the "P" list is longer than the "C" list. I find that more boring than instructive or helpful. Instead, I choose to focus on just the "pros". I created a little handbook of reminders for myself to help me "snap out of it" when I'm feeling low, and get on with life.

I entitled it *My Positive Past (So Far)*. It's simply a small photo album that I purchased at the local drug store, and it holds one hundred 3" X 5" photos in the plastic sleeves. I also bought one hundred 3" X 5" index cards and began filling out each one, not all at the same time, but over the years. As I thought of something I really liked or admired about myself (yes, we're allowed to do that!) or something really good that happened in my life, I jotted it down on one of the index cards and slipped it into a sleeve in the photo album.

I'll share some of the messages with you here, in no particular pecking order, just to give you a sense of it:

o I have a good telephone voice
o I enjoy singing and joined a chorus where I could sing on stage
o I understand the importance of saving and try to be wise with my money
o I am not shy about dressing up in outrageous Halloween costumes
o I volunteer a lot, especially when no one else will

- I am a frequent blood donor
- I never go to a party empty-handed
- I am determined to figure things out and don't give up easily
- I try to be a good listener and not force my own agenda
- I love to make people laugh
- I wrote a self-help book to help people ease their health challenges

Whenever I get down on myself or I feel I'm in a helpless, hopeless situation, I pull out my little "handbook". I remind myself that I *do* have some positive traits, that I *have* achieved some worthwhile goals, that I *don't* deserve the invisible mental "L" I've placed on my forehead when things don't work out for me the way I'd like them to.

Try it for yourself. Everyone has *something* positive or unique about themselves to write down. For now, this may be your only chance to toot your horn (even though weakly) to help you rise above your struggles. If you learn to expect optimism, you're more likely to achieve it.

So, take advantage of it. These cards are for you, to share with no one but yourself. There is no asset or trait too insignificant to write down, no accomplishment too meager to record. Sometimes, what you perceive at first as a "negative" attribute can actually be a "positive", a blessing in disguise. It's all about wanting what you have—not having whatever you want.

Take the case of the woman, who, after a lifetime of jokes and off-color comments about her substantial bosom, went to a doctor to ask for a "painless" reduction in size. (In order to get the full effect of what transpired, I want you to go and get a calculator now. Then, follow along with me, typing in the numbers as I instruct you. Go ahead. I'll wait (... ... ... tick-tock, tick-tock).

Okay. Now, back to the story. The doctor took a tape measure and measured her chest, just to get a starting point. He found it to be sixty-nine inches around. (*NOW, TYPE IN **69**.*)

The doctor said, "Yes, I agree. That's too large for your frame." He went into his desk drawer and took out a bottle of pills. He said, "I want you to take two of these pills every two hours for two weeks and then come back to see me. (*TYPE IN **222** RIGHT NEXT TO THE FIRST NUMBER.*)

She returned to the doctor in two weeks to be measured again. Lo and behold, she was down to fifty-one inches! (*NOW, TYPE IN **51** NEXT TO THE OTHER TWO NUMBERS.*)

The doctor was thrilled with her progress, but the woman wanted to get even smaller, no matter what it took. So, she asked if she could take the rest of the pills in the bottle. The doctor vehemently shook his head "no", saying that it would be purely experimental. He couldn't even begin to imagine what might happen if she took all of the pills.

But, she was adamant so, reluctantly, the doctor said, "Okay. Take the rest of these pills and come back to see me in eight weeks. But, I warn you: I don't know what might happen. The worst possible thing in the world could happen." (*TYPE IN **X 8** = AFTER ALL THE NUMBERS. YOUR ANSWER SHOULD BE 55378008.*)

The woman came back eight weeks later, and

sure enough—the worst possible thing that could have happened, did. When the doctor measured her again, he found she was **55378008**. (*TURN THE CALCULATOR UPSIDE DOWN NOW AND READ WHAT IT SAYS. YOU'LL SEE THAT YOUR ANSWER SPELLS OUT "**BOOBLESS**".*)

So, you see? Acknowledge your assets and accept them. Things could always be worse!

- SEVENTEEN -

Halloween: One of My Favorite Holidays

Halloween is one of the holidays I like best in the entire year. It's a day of make-believe, of transforming yourself into someone or something apart from who you really are. It's a great opportunity to take your mind off your troubles and be a carefree kid again, even if just for a day. Call it a "Mental Health Day", a time to take a break and refocus your energies toward something other than your health problems.

At the last office I worked in, we maintained a tradition of dressing up and working in costume for Halloween each year. There would be a prize for the best one, voted on by the entire staff. I won five out of the six years I worked there. (I held back the first year, just to get a feel of the place.) Then, on Halloween night, my next-door neighbor and I would sit on our lawn chairs in front of our homes, waiting for the neighborhood kids to come trick-or-treating. Some of the parents seemed just as interested in taking a picture of me as they did of their own kids.

 C3 ❧ ⱤRℰꙨ ❦ ℰꙨ

One Halloween, I dressed up as a California Freeway. I wore an all-black sweatshirt and pants onto which I had sewn a white, dotted line made of rectangular, felt patches. The dotted line went all the way up each pant leg, and then merged to a single dotted line up to my neckline. I used clown-white grease paint to continue the dotted line from my chin to my hairline.

On my head, I wore a rectangular-shaped box (that my bank checks had come in) covered in green felt and sewn onto a headband. *Recreation Area* was printed on the front of the box. Attached to it was a string of miniature, white Christmas lights surrounding the perimeter of the road sign. The electric cord ran down my shirt and into my pants. I operated the lights by flipping on the switch from a battery pack concealed in my pants pocket.

I attached little toy cars to the front of the costume, as well as small, furry animal toys (road kill) and even a plastic picnic fork, glued at an angle over the dotted line. (A "fork in the road", get it?) I glued on variously-shaped, felt traffic signs on which I had printed such words as *Soft Shoulder, Dangerous Curves* and *Dead End*. These were strategically placed on the body of the costume.

C3 ❧ ⱤRℰꙨ ❦ ℰꙨ

Another year, I came as One Nightstand (or the double entendre, "one night stand"). To give the costume some shape, I took a large, circular, plastic deli tray to form the tabletop and slit the tray halfway across. Then I cut a hole in the center of it for my head to slip through. I draped a round tablecloth (with an opening cut in the center for my head) over the tray that now encircled my neck. Over the tablecloth, I wore a white, short, tabletop piece (like a doily with the center cut out) which extended from around my neck to just over my shoulders.

On top of the white doily tabletop, I glued on a little plastic alarm clock, an ashtray with two cigarette butts (lipstick on one), two plastic champagne glasses (one overturned, with lipstick on it), an open book entitled *"Everything You Need to Know About Sex"*, a clear plastic bottle containing red pompoms and labeled *Viagra*, and a condom in its wrapper. On my head, I wore a lampshade with fringe and a pull chain to complete the nightstand image.

જ્ઞ ૐ ૱ૐ ૹ ૱

One Halloween, I took a man's XXL-size, flesh-colored, pullover shirt (which, on me, became a dress) and glued on, randomly all over the shirt, various sizes of sponges and mirrors. On each sponge, I wrote the word, *Me*, with a felt-tip marker. I pinned an *I'm the Greatest* blue ribbon award on my chest and then threaded a length of twine through a roll of paper towels. The roll hung down around my neck on the twine like a big, absorbent necklace.

All evening, I gazed lovingly at myself into a hand-held mirror on a cord that hung around my neck. A little sign on the flip side proclaimed, *It's all about me!* I entitled my costume "Self-Absorbed".

∞✦∞∞✦∞

My "piece d'resistance" costume, however, was an X-ray Machine (a "natural", after all my medical experiences). I acquired a giant, empty, toilet paper carton from my local WalMart and cut out holes at the top and sides for my head and arms to go through. I covered the whole box with white Contac paper and trimmed out all the openings using "man's best friend"—duct tape.

On the front of the box, I fashioned a little door that opened by pulling on a round, wooden doorknob screwed to it. The door opened to reveal a sheer, black, cloth screen. Behind the sheer cloth, I fastened the torso of a glow-in-the-dark, plastic skeleton to hang down inside the box in front of me. Another black, sheer screen behind it sandwiched the skeleton in place. Wearing a long-sleeved, black pullover, I was virtually invisible behind the skeleton. Around the door opening, I secured a row of miniature, white Christmas lights that I worked from a battery pack in my pants pocket. When I flipped on the switch for the lights, the scary skeleton was revealed. (*Woooooooo!!!*)

I completed the costume by attaching a long, narrow tray to the front of the door. The tray held a couple x-rays of my veterinarian friend's cat, Owen. I labeled the tray appropriately—*Cat Scan.*

That year my friend, Sheila, called the local newspaper to tell them about my costume creations. A reporter called me and did a telephone interview and then sent a photographer out to my home. But, I never expected my costume to occupy the front page of the newspaper that weekend (*above* the fold, no less), along with a full-blown article about me beneath the picture! My phone didn't stop ringing for a week.

C3 ❧ CR80 ❧ 80

There *are* some people, though, who just don't care for all the fun and festivities of the holiday. In fact, I understand that Jehovah's Witnesses don't celebrate Halloween at all. (I guess they just don't like people ringing their doorbells and annoying them.)

But, I hope you try to do something fun for yourself next Halloween. You'll be surprised how it takes your mind off your troubles for a while.

- EIGHTEEN -

How the Ducks and Others Helped Me Pass the Time

As I was healing from surgery, I didn't have a whole lot of stamina or desire to do much from the beginning. But, as I plodded down that road to recovery, I found myself getting bored, itching for something to do to break up the monotony of the long days.

Paging through one of those mail-order catalogs everyone receives, an item called "Resin Porch Ducks" caught my eye. One white duck was about eighteen inches tall and the other stood about ten inches tall. The price tag included nine different holiday outfits. There was one for "New Year's Eve", complete with top hat and tails, another for "Valentine's Day", "St. Patrick's Day", "Easter", "Fourth of July", "Halloween", "Thanksgiving", "Christmas" and "Birthday". (I suppose that last one pays for itself if you have a large family.)

When the carton containing the ducks appeared on my front porch, I found they were as cute as the catalog advertisement had claimed. I immediately installed them on my front lawn, and they became the talk of the neighborhood as I changed their costumes month after month.

A man who lives nearby (the resident "Mr. Mom" in the neighborhood) frequently comes by on his motor scooter with one or both of his kids in tow. They visit the ducks at least five days a week, sometimes even more than once a day, at the children's urging. I began to see that these ducks served a purpose beyond being a curiosity. The little kids were beginning to learn about the various holidays.

I got to thinking: I wondered if I could fashion costumes for the other months of the year, even though there might not be an official holiday for the month. So, while I was home healing from my breast cancer and knee surgeries, I set off on a mission to fill in those missing months with costumes. With the aid of my trusty sewing machine, simple patterns that I designed, and some fabric and "accessories", the ducks now have a full wardrobe of costume changes.

I began with "April Showers", making little, yellow slickers and rain hats, and then glued a tiny umbrella onto one of the slickers. For "Cinco de Mayo" I fashioned sombreros, serapes, a chili pepper necklace and a tiny guitar on a length of yarn to hang around the little duck's neck (ducks don't have arms, you know). Also for May, I followed with "Graduation", creating caps and gowns and diplomas. Then came "June Bride", complete with a veil, lace gown, a silk flower bouquet hung from her neck and even a ball and chain for her little mate, made from a golf ball painted black. For August, I created "Vacation Time", making swimsuits and sunhats, accessorizing with sunglasses, a camera and binoculars. Of course, September is "Back to School" month, so the large duck sports a cheerleader outfit with pompoms and megaphone, and the little duck wears a beanie, geeky little eyeglasses and a school bag of books (hung around his neck). Combining fabric scraps I had at home with various accessories purchased from the local dollar store, the costumes hardly cost me anything.

And here's an interesting sidebar about the two little neighborhood children. Instead of asking their dad to take them to see the ducks during May, Mr. Mom told me they asked to visit "the graduates". So, in the process, I've actually helped to create a learning tool for these two little kids.

This pastime has begun to take on a life of its own. I find myself keeping an eye out for obscure holidays so I can create costumes to celebrate them alongside the traditional ones. People tell me they look forward to the costume changes, too, so that's what saves me from being labeled the neighborhood weirdo.

Friends have made costume donations to help expand the ducks' wardrobes. One neighbor telephoned to suggest that the small duck needed a little more dressing up for January. So, to be in balance with the larger one's ice skating outfit, I quickly fashioned a poncho and earmuffs for the little guy. Another neighbor said he even was tempted to steal the little one, take him along on one of this out-of-town business trips and send me a post card from the two of them! (And you think *I'm* weird?) Subconsciously, too, I'm sure I'm paying silent tribute to that venerable insurance duck whose coverage has been so good to me over the years.

Visual aids, neighborhood entertainment and

insurance promos aside, it's been a great way for me to keep from "quacking up", you might say, while passing the time as I continued to heal. It also helped me refocus on things other than medical care or treatments. (My record one particular month was having *nineteen* medical appointments.) Believe me when I say that I needed to find another outlet, something else on which to focus my time and attention.

CR૭⮟CRᴁᴐᴗᴆᴐ

After undergoing foot surgery eight times, I had formed a friendship with my podiatrist and his wife who worked in his office.   Each time I was home "cooling my heels" from those surgeries, I busied myself in crafts to pass the time.

One year close to Christmas, I decided to make a small holiday ornament for their office door. I bought a twig wreath, the size of a small grapefruit, at a craft store. I fastened on a bare, rubber foot (normally used in making dolls) to hang down within the wreath. I parted the big toe from the rest of the foot with my utility knife, leaving room to "bandage" the toe. I completed the ornament by wiring on a sprig of mistletoe around the bottom edge of the twigs, along with a bright red ribbon. My creation: "Mistle*TOE*".

Later on, I immersed myself in needlepoint, but not using just ordinary, store-bought needlework kits. I noticed that my podiatrist had several cartoon prints decorating his examining room walls relating to feet, so that gave me an idea. Using graph paper, I made my own patterns and created a needlepoint design of the Tic Tac Toe grid. I worked in the "X" in three sections of the grid but replaced the traditional "O" with a toe stitched into the design in the three diagonal spaces.

Then, I ran a length of red yarn diagonally over the toes to win the "Tic Tac *TOE*" game.

My final needlepoint project was a design I created of a "*TOE* Truck", a red truck with a winch on the rear of it. Attached to the hoist was a big toe. On the door of the truck, I took thin, black yarn and worked in the podiatrist's phone number.

I healed from the foot surgeries finally, the doctor's office walls were filled, and my craft projects came to an end for a while.

CB&-CR80-&80

From crafts, I graduated to computer games. Solitaire occupied a good portion of my time, but I abandoned that even though I had reached a "personal best" of almost 22,000 points in just over sixty seconds. (Ahhh...I take my victories from wherever I can get them!)

A co-worker of mine at the time gave me a computer Scrabble game to occupy me while I was home healing from the knee and breast cancer surgeries. It completely diverted my attention from Solitaire and has captivated my interest to this day. Not only do I now possess a fabulous vocabulary of words I'll probably never use, but it greatly helped me improve my finger dexterity following the subsequent carpal tunnel surgeries.

In the solitude of my computer room, I'd find myself playing far into the night, and venting frequently after losing my turn on a Scrabble word challenge. I'd cuss out the computer when I disagreed with a word *it* had used, especially after denying a word of *mine* that I knew darn well existed. Now, I don't presume to know *everything*, but it annoyed me that the computer could "get away with" selecting such words as the name of an ancient, no-longer-existing foreign coin, for example, from a place like "Lower Slobovia", or the like. *That's* the kind of word that ticked me off and got me talking out loud.

But, it was futile, you see, because there's no way to have the final say in a word dispute with the computer (except to hit "Control", "Alt", Delete). My protests *have* served to bring my low blood pressure up to normal, however; so, there *is* an upside to the exercise, after all. (And, I *still* believe that foreign words have never been allowed in Scrabble.)

CʒᏽᏭCᎡᏇᎧᏽᏭᏵᏬ

Another activity you can try yourself (which won't do battle with your blood pressure) is to spend a little time browsing through the hospital gift shop if you happen to arrive too early for a medical appointment. I've found that it's a good place to kill time, and it beats sitting in a doctor's waiting room, touching all those magazines sick people have handled before you. (Warning! Don't ever lick your finger and then use that finger to turn the magazine page at the top. That's where everybody licks, then touches the pages. There's no telling what you can pick up. Turn it from halfway down or from the bottom. Hardly anybody turns pages from there.)

A hospital gift shop is a nice place to find unique presents, too, perhaps buying a little get-well gift for yourself (an automatic "cheer-me-upper") or one to tuck away for the future to brighten someone else's day. There aren't salespeople hovering around, trying to make a sale, and it's much less crowded than going to the mall. Even if you don't buy anything, you can use the time to build your strength and get your "land legs" back with a little walking, combined with window shopping. (Be careful that you don't knock anything off the shelves while you're strolling, though.)

ᘓᘔ᥊ᘓᘓᘔᗜ᥊ᘓᘔ

If you really have no talent for (or interest in) crafts, cards or board games, or if you're simply not well enough yet for physical activity like taking a walk, there still is something you can do. It's not meant to isolate you—no, just the opposite. It will help you get started. It needs no batteries and requires absolutely no assembly before use. It's called: stimulating your mind.

This activity is one hundred per cent sedentary but will help keep the cobwebs out of your brain. You can just stand/sit/lie there comfortably while you're resting and turn your mind loose, letting your creative juices flow.

Try making up a joke or a riddle. Here's a couple I just made up to get you started:

Why did the veterinarian prescribe Viagra to the sick snake? Because he had "a reptile dysfunction".

Or, how about this one?

What do you call it when a prince passes gas loudly? "Air apparent".

If you're not feeling particularly clever yet, try your hand at creating an anagram. You already have all the parts needed. Using all the letters in your own name, switch them around until they spell something else. For example, an anagram using all the letters of my full name—Annette L. Langer—is "elegant lantern". (Isn't that cute?)

Experiment with others' names, too. Have fun with it.

 GR*ORED*GEO

You'll find that these exercises and others you devise will help to pass the time as you're healing. Hopefully, at some point, you'll be strong enough to throw that notepad across the room on your own power and then move on to more meaningful activities.

– NINETEEN –

It's the Year to Volunteer!

A brief article appearing in my local newspaper one day invited participation in a program offered by the local police department called the "Citizens Police Academy". Various facets of law enforcement procedures would be covered over the fourteen weeks in once-a-week classroom meetings. Topics ranged from patrol functions (including canine patrol) to investigations, crime prevention, narcotics, S.W.A.T. team duties and, in general, the importance of public involvement in the policing process. I eagerly signed up for it, hoping my unusual medical history wouldn't eliminate me from consideration. I had to obtain consent from my "health care provider" (who just told me to use my head and not take any unnecessary risks), and I had to agree to a background check.

The class was comprised of about twenty-five adult participants. (A separate class for mature, older teens was offered during the summertime.) The training coordinator of the Citizens Academy was another good-looking man in uniform, whom I'll just refer to as Sgt. "Hottie". Each week, we received our instruction from various police officers, an assistant district attorney and even a superior court judge.

One of the highlights of the course was a "ride-along" with a patrol officer. The assignment was intended to run no longer than four hours (shorter, if you got bored...or scared). I was so "captivated" (pun intended) by the events which occurred that night that I stayed with my officer (and his canine) through his entire work shift. We logged fifty-three miles on the odometer by the end of the evening, just cruising around town.

We made a number of traffic stops, looked for someone evading an arrest warrant, and conducted a search for a minor reported to be drunk and on drugs in a pool hall. We responded to a radio report of a jewelry store robbery in progress at the local shopping mall and raced there at breakneck speed on the freeway. (The canine in the caged enclosure behind me went nuts the whole way because he knew he was going to work soon). We arrested a drunk on a public street and followed another patrol car to transport him to jail to sleep it off (since we couldn't take on passengers). All this occurred in just one night in my sleepy ol' home town!

At the conclusion of the fourteen-week Academy training, the Chief of Police presented each of us with a completion certificate in a graduation ceremony, followed by a catered dinner. One of my classmates, an older lady, lamented that her only regret in completing the course was that she wouldn't be able to look at Sgt. "Hottie" anymore.

ᎰᎣᏈᎲᎲᎣᏈᎲᎣᏈᎥ

Since then, I've participated as a volunteer at various police functions. On our own, another private citizen and I did a fundraiser to purchase bulletproof vests for the police department's three canines. (Why not? They're at risk, too.) We held a press conference with reporters from the regional newspapers to publicize the event and then secured a booth at one of the local street fairs in town. We designed flyers to distribute at the fair, for which I obtained free printing from a neighborhood printer. I also took photos of each of the three police canines and got another commercial print shop in town to convert these photos into life-size, cardboard cut-outs, again at no charge.

We used these eye-catching, free-standing posters to decorate our booth at the fair. We collected donations from the public at the event and then secured contributions for a few months after that from many of the local businesses around town. Our efforts were so successful that, ultimately, we raised enough money to purchase all three assault vests, with roughly $10,000.00 left over for future vest replacement! (We even received a commendation from the Mayor at a city council meeting, flanked by the canines sporting their new protective vests.)

At S.W.A.T. team all-day training exercises, I've role-played with the team in various simulated rescue and assault situations, including crisis negotiation. Sometimes, I play the suspect and other times, the victim. In one scenario, played out in an old abandoned building, I portrayed the bad guy (my favorite role). I hid out in a five-foot high metal gym locker with only a bottle of water and my radium-dial wristwatch to keep me company. Finally, after a half-hour, one of the police canines sniffed me out of my hiding place. I was extracted from the locker, made to kneel down and then be handcuffed. The more I struggled, the tighter the cuffs got. (Tuck this tidbit away for future reference.)

Afterwards, the S.W.A.T. team leader thanked me for my efforts, saying, "I'll bet this brought you back to old your high school days", intimating that I probably got stuffed in a gym locker at least once back then.

But, what really struck me funny was watching one of the canine handlers place a circle of yellow "Do Not Cross" police caution tape around a fresh pile of dog poop he found in the building as we were leaving. (One of the excited canines just couldn't wait to get outside to "dispose of" the evidence, I guess.)

During some of these training exercises, we use handguns containing simulated ammunition (that's live ammo, but reduced-energy 9mm "marking" cartridges). I wear a bulletproof vest like the rest of the S.W.A.T. team members, as well as protective gear to cover my head and throat (since they'll be shooting at me, as well). At the conclusion of each scenario, the team leader gives feedback to the team on their effectiveness. He checks the number of "hits" the other volunteer and I took by counting the half-dozen or so colored markers left on our vests, helmets, etc., including one on my exposed ring finger the first time I got hit. (I suppose you'd call that "taking one *from* the team" instead of for the team.) Since that baptism by fire(power), however, I've learned to wear protective gloves. Now, I've just got to work on my own aim. The one and only direct shot I took at the S.W.A.T. team charging toward me that time struck a nearby bench instead. (Talk about misdirected adrenaline!)

I've been formally accepted now as a "Volunteer in Police Service", the official title for what I do. I can spend as little as eight hours a month as a Police Volunteer to as much time as I'm able to give. I still role play at S.W.A.T. team training, but have some additional duties, too. These run the gamut from fingerprinting people whose jobs require it (like child-care workers and liquor license applicants) to actual street duty in a patrol car with a Volunteer partner (in a full uniform, but without a weapon, of course). We're trained in basic first aid and CPR and how to use the two-way radio and on-board computer in the patrol car. We direct traffic at accident scenes, do home vacation patrol checks and transport evidence or equipment, when requested. We're the "eyes and ears" of the sworn police officers and assist in any way directed by them, including just being a uniformed presence at high school dances, the various street fairs and other events in town.

ᏣᏅ•ᏣᏁᎦᏲ•ᏋᏊ

I also volunteer occasionally with the local chapter of Habitat for Humanity, an international, nonprofit organization that builds homes for low-income working families. Eligible families are selected to purchase three- or four-bedroom homes at less than market value, and interest free. In consideration, each family must "partner with Habitat" and perform five hundred hours of "sweat equity" labor in helping to build their own home, alongside other volunteer workers (like me). Volunteers are taught simple building tasks and otherwise assist the "real" construction workers on the site who handle the more exacting duties.

I don't have any real building skills (other than knowing that the pointy end of the nail goes into the wood). And, I'm very careful so I don't re-injure myself in any way, of course. But, Habitat assures volunteers that there's a job of some sort for everyone, even if it's just working in their office rather than at the job site.

I've taken inventory of all building materials at the site, recording the numbers for the site superintendent. I've pulled nails out of wooden braces in the newly-framed structures (holding my breath and hoping the house wouldn't fall down around me as I removed the last temporary brace). I've carried lumber to other workers, cut lumber with an electric table saw (no kidding), hammered in nails to construct framing, painted, leveled fence posts to be bolted, coiled up extension cords and covered up building materials with tarps at the day's end.

No job is too small, and all efforts are welcomed. It's a good feeling to help less fortunate people realize their dream of home ownership and be able to physically play a small part in it. It's also another way of getting outside yourself to focus on something other than your own challenges.

ॐ֍ॐ֍ॐ

I volunteer my time and talent at the nonprofit community theatre in town and at other theatres in the area, including a nearby community opera company. My duties have varied from singing on stage with the chorus to performing some of the behind-the-scenes jobs, such as music librarian, fundraiser, cast party host, theatre usher, and even concession stand operator at intermission. In exchange for these minor duties, I'm able to see every drama, musical and opera in the area, and at no cost.

There are many things you can get involved in while healing in order to refocus your energies (even if they're meager at first) to help you look beyond your health problems. You have the opportunity to meet a lot of wonderful people who are only too happy to receive your services, to accommodate you, and allow you to do *what* you can, *when* you can. Everybody wins!

- TWENTY -

Losing Your Job, Not Your Life

My last job afforded me three weeks' annual vacation, plus five personal days and seven holidays. That's twenty-seven paid days off a year. Let's be generous and call it four weeks, in total. During the period mid-January through early March of the following year, I was absent for various medical reasons a total of one hundred fifty-nine days, including arriving late and leaving work early for medical appointments. That's about six months of absence during a fifteen-month period, give or take.

From an employer's standpoint, that made me a liability. To compound the problem, my company's home office decided to close our location and transfer the workload to one of our offices in another city where salaries were less than what we were being paid. In determining the order in which employees should be laid off over the next several months, management decided that those least valuable to the company would be the first to go. Translation: "Bye, Bye, Annette."

Now, some may file this under the "Why me?" category, lamenting, "I never asked to be sick or injured." In the six years I worked for that firm, I rarely took any sick days, other than in that final year or so. In fact, I scheduled all my medical appointments early or late in the day in order to minimize my absence from the job.

But, to quote Donald Trump, "It's nothing personal—it's just business", and I was one of the first to be laid off. Sure, my feelings were hurt in the beginning. Whose wouldn't be? But, I forced myself to look forward and just chalked it up to "that's life".

When thinking about major upheaval during one's lifetime, however, job loss is right up there with marriage, divorce, moving to a new home, major illness and death. It is a stressful time of life, to say the least. But, many times, the only control over a situation that we have is the manner in which we respond to it. (Is it a hangnail, or is it a train wreck?) Losing one's job falls somewhere in between the two.

So, boo-hoo! There is no lasting payoff in staying bitter or hurt, in bemoaning the past or why it happened. It just happened, and that's that. Even Mark Twain said, "Don't go around saying the world owes you a living. The world owes you nothing. It was here first."

 CZ ஃ CRED ஃ ED

I once received an e-mail from a friend recounting a young girl's letter to her parents that detailed her current predicament. It shows how humor can help you step back and see things in a new way. The letter went something like this:

> "Dear Mom and Dad,
>
> I'm sorry I haven't kept in touch, but my dorm burned down and my computer got fried. I'm out of the hospital now and am able to write a little.
>
> I've moved in with my new boyfriend, Ahmed. He's been a treasure through all of this, and I don't know what I would have done without him. We're living in a commune where we grow the marijuana he needs for his glaucoma. How sad it is to see him suffer with this and with AIDS, too. No one deserves that.
>
> On a brighter note, I know how much you've always wanted a grandchild, so I'm so happy to announce that I'm pregnant. Be happy for us!
>
> Love, Susie
>
> P.S. There was no fire, I'm perfectly healthy, and I'm not pregnant. I don't even *have* a boyfriend. But, I did fail chemistry and biology, and when you receive my grades, I just wanted to make sure you keep it all in perspective."

०३ॐ०३४०ॐ४०

The weight you assign to a problem can give it disproportionate value in the grand scheme of things, if you let it. (Remember my story of the two young women at the zoo at the beginning of the book?) Very few occurrences in life will be "the end of the world" (except the end of the world, of course). In the meantime, you can exercise more control over a situation than you ever before believed, just by how you view it. That's not hooey, it's "true-y"!

If a guy went to the movies and a tall guy sat in front of him, he was pretty much screwed. He could sit there, be miserable and take it, or he could move. Maya Angelou said, "Making a living is not making a life." Your job *isn't* your life, although many people treat it as if it were.

The only rational choice when losing one's job is to deal with it constructively. Otherwise, all the energy, time and brainpower you have are channeled into feeling sorry for yourself, just like the short guy at the movies, rather than into moving forward and planning that next step. Plus, taking a defeatist attitude makes your shoulders droop a little, and that's not a good look. Remember, body language is powerful and can speak volumes to your next prospective employer.

Speaking of job prospects, you can still ready yourself for future employment while you're healing, even if it just means working on getting back your positive mental attitude. Here's an example.

I had been receiving treatment at the same physical therapy facility for well over a year (at first for my knee injuries and later on for the carpal tunnel repair and then for Lymphodema). I had the good fortune to work with all fifteen of the physical therapists and aides there at one time or another. I tried to be cheerful and pleasant toward them at each session, no matter how I was feeling. I knew that all they ever saw every day, all day long, were people who were struggling and in pain. If I could brighten their days while they were helping me, we'd all win.

When I walked in, every one of them called me by my name, and that's no small feat, considering the number of patients who passed through their doors on a daily basis. And speaking of "feet", I even loaned one of the therapists one of my surgical shoes to wear while she was recovering from a foot injury, herself. I could see that my gesture really touched her.

One physical therapist I worked with for a few months was leaving to move back East. A going-away party for her was planned at a local restaurant, and she encouraged me to attend. I sat at the long banquet table with most of the employees of the physical therapy facility, as well as the owner and her husband. But other than a few boyfriends and spouses sprinkled in, I soon realized that I seemed to be one of the only patients there.

The next time I went in for my treatment, the owner took me aside and told me that her husband had said to her after the party, "Now, *there's* someone you should hire."

Then she said to me, "When the time is right and you've healed, let's talk."

෬෪ঌ෬ඣ෪ঌ෬

You never know where that next window is going to open after a door is slammed shut. You can make a positive impact wherever you go.

EPILOGUE

I hope these pages have brought a smile to your face. At the risk of sounding "preachy" or "sicklier than thou," I'll end by being serious for a minute and offering some advice from my heart.

I'm not saying that I'm carefree and lighthearted all the time. I wouldn't be human if I were. (In fact, there have been times that I've had more pains than a house made of windows.) But there's no point in compounding a problem by being maudlin or getting despondent over it, bemoaning the fact that you're sick in the first place. In other words, you already have a problem. Why create a *second* problem—worrying about the first one?

Coping with challenges in life is all about making informed choices. That's what puts us at the top of the food chain (that, and possessing opposable thumbs, of course). It's not just a knee-jerk reaction to outside elements. You have the opportunity to choose how to handle any situation, to heal your mind and your heart, even if you can't always control the forces to heal your body.

Whether you're reading this book yourself or having someone read it to you, you're still making the choice to take it in. Learn to re-focus your energies, and it'll work like a shot in the arm—a shot of *hope*, not dope. The healing begins when you make a real effort to get outside of your health challenge—in other words, not "become" your illness.

I once knew a young man who had developed cancer three times in his life. When he met people for the first time, he'd introduce himself by saying something like, "Hi, I'm So-and-So. I've had cancer three times." Maybe it was his way of breaking the ice with strangers, but it really just put most people off. It's hard enough to be stricken with a serious illness or injury. But, to compound it by making it a primary focus in one's life slows the healing and brings a person down even further, dragging others down in the process.

In his book, "The Healing Power of Humor", author Allen Klein says, "It is of vital importance that as a patient, as a care-giver, or as someone who is concerned about the welfare of the patient, we remain uplifted and keep a positive attitude that includes hope, joy and laughter even during the most trying times. Humor gives people that choice. It shows them that they do not have to be so stuck in their predicaments. It shows them that they do not have to be blinded by pain and suffering."

When you live with chronic illness or pain, there is a tendency to believe that it's your job to be sick. It's what you "do" for most of your waking hours. But, through humor, you can give both your mind and heart a holiday from that job. And *you* can be in charge of the length of that holiday. You may not be able to control your pain, but you can find ways to gain power over your suffering. Allow humor in to help you find the "positives" in your life. You need it to heal.

Many years ago I was about to take my first college midterm exam, and I was overcome with the fear that I wouldn't pass it. I was older than the rest of the students and lacked the confidence to keep up with them. I kept saying over and over, "I won't pass! I won't pass!" But it was my own dear mother, in her infinite wisdom (and characteristic style of humor), who gently chided me for my outlook.

"Stop being so negative, saying you *won't* pass," she said. "You've got to learn to think positive: Say, 'I *will* fail! I *will* fail!'"

Through her own use of humor, she got me to see that negative energy never accomplishes anything. Ever.

Michael Jordan is quoted as saying, "I've missed more than nine thousand shots in my career. I've lost almost three hundred games. Twenty-six times I've been trusted to take the game-winning shot and missed. I've failed over and over and over again in my life. And that is why I succeed."

If you are at all spiritual and believe in God or just a higher power, you will understand and accept that your mind and body are gifts entrusted to you, to be taken back when it's time. In the meantime, you have the responsibility to cooperate in your healing, even if it takes what seems like forever.

Kathy Cordova quotes an old Indian proverb in her book, "Let Go, Let Miracles Happen: The Art of Spiritual Surrender", that says, "Call on God, but row away from the rocks."

You have to do your part, too. You can't stop living because medical issues stall you from your normal activities, temporarily or even permanently. A favorite expression of mine is "Heaven doesn't want me yet, and Hell's afraid I'll take over. So, I guess I'd just better keep on living."

But, Ralph Waldo Emerson said it best, I think: "Guard well your spare moments. They are like uncut diamonds. Discard them and their value will never be known. Improve them and they will become the brightest gems in a useful life." (Way to go, Ralph!)

I have a friend who suddenly lost the sight in one eye for no discernable reason. After several medication changes, treatments and surgery, there's still no measurable improvement in her vision. But, despite these efforts and their disappointing results, Donna continues to cope with this major setback in her life. She attends lectures and seminars when she can and listens to books on audio tape from the local library in order to keep herself in the loop. She continues to challenge and stimulate her mind, despite the physical setback she is facing.

While you are healing, use this time to discover the alterations you can make in your own life to keep you moving forward. And, let humor guide you on your path. There are things you can discover to enrich your life, things you maybe never thought in a million years you could or would do. If anyone would have predicted that I'd switch careers from court reporter to office manager to travel planner and then immerse myself almost full time in volunteer work, I'd never have believed it. If anyone told me I'd be making costumes for myself or for resin garden ducks, for Heaven's sake, then "crazy" doesn't even begin to cover my reaction. And, if anyone told me I'd be writing a *book* about all this—well, don't even get me started! You already possess the tools to help you move forward to overcome the obstacles in your life. You just have to remember how to use them again. Change your focus! Change your life!

I hope you take something from these pages to make your own and to help you through whatever personal challenges you face. And, I sincerely hope that you allow humor to accompany you on your journey. If you enjoyed this book, please recommend it to your friends. If you hated it, then encourage your enemies to buy it. (At least it will have brought you *some* satisfaction!)

Helen Keller once said, "We would never learn to be brave and patient if there were only joy in the world." How perfect a way to grow. I had dinner with friends recently in a Chinese restaurant. When I cracked open my fortune cookie at the end of the meal, the message inside read: *Think about the good things you have today.* How perfect a way to end this book.

ABOUT THE AUTHOR

Annette Langer grew up in and around metropolitan Chicago where she graduated Magna Cum Laude from Loyola University with a degree in Counseling Psychology. She spent a long career holding various positions with the Federal Government before reaching her ultimate goal—early retirement! Langer then prepared herself for her "life after" and went back to school, training for a second career as a travel agent, work that she enjoyed for more than twenty years after that.

After living practically her entire life in the Midwest, Langer decided to pull up stakes in 1998 and head to California where she had always wanted to live. She knew she had made the right decision after seeing an advertisement in a travel magazine. It read: *The sun comes up in the east as an obligation. Then the sun heads for California out of blatant self-interest. The sun is no dummy. California: find yourself here...*

Retired now from the wacky world of travel planning, Langer has immersed herself in volunteer work and has renewed her love for writing, becoming an active member of the Tri-Valley Writers Association. She resides happily in the San Francisco Bay Area where she continues to meet life's challenges, but in better weather.

Langer is currently working on her next book entitled, "A Funny Thing Happened to Me on the Way to the World: Diary of a Fearless Travel Agent". Watch for it!

This and other quality books are available from

OverLookedBooks

Visit us online at:
www.overlookedbooks.com

Printed in the United States
44639LVS00002B/496-570

9 781595 940254